TONY BATES has had a lifelong interest in natural history, and has lived in Dorset since 1971. He is a keen amateur nature photographer and lecturer, and has helped set up a number of conservation projects for the Dorset Wildlife Trust. He is currently a Council member, Chairman of the Promotion and Education Committee and the Higher Hyde Heath Nature Reserve Management Committee.

KEVIN COOK first became interested in wildlife thirty years ago, when he worked as a conservation volunteer in Gloucester and Somerset. Since graduating he has worked as a professional conservationist, as manager of an ancient woodland in Essex, and as a senior countryside officer. Since 1984 he has been Head Warden of the Dorset Wildlife Trust's Brownsea Island Nature Reserve, adding to his experience of habitat management.

BILL COPLAND is a former Council member and a past Chairman of the Conservation and Marine Committees of the Dorset Wildlife Trust. He was south-west Regional Officer of the Nature Conservancy Council and, later, environmental education adviser for Dorset County Council. He served on the Wessex Regional Committee of the National Trust for over ten years, and is an experienced author and editor.

BOB GIBBONS has been involved with nature conservation and natural history most of his life. After ten years working for the Nature Conservancy Council and the Wildlife Trusts, he became a freelance photographer, author, tour leader and ecological consultant. He has written and/or provided the photographs for about thirty books, including the highly acclaimed *Flora Britannica*. He lives in Dorset and travels throughout the world leading tours and taking photographs.

LESLEY HASKINS became fascinated with heathland following a nature walk over Talbot Heath, and she went on to make its history the subject of her PhD. thesis. Her studies brought her into contact with the scientists and conservationists working at Furzebrook Research Station, and she is currently Deputy Chairman of the Dorset Wildlife Trust and Chairman of the Conservation and Scientific Committee.

ANNE HORSFA⁻ botanist, photo₂ detailed botanica valuable evidence war. She is particu the Dorset flora an woodlands.

COLIN VARNDELL first became interested in natural history during a childhood spent in west Dorset. Since 1989 he has devoted his time to wildlife photography, and his collection of over 80,000 colour transparencies depicting birds, mammals, reptiles, amphibians, butterflies, dragonflies, moths, invertebrates, wild flowers, fungi, mosses, lichens, landscape and the weather. His first book, *Wildlife in the West Country*, was published in 1994.

SARAH WELTON moved to Dorset in 1971 after graduating in Zoology from the University of Wales. She worked for the Dorset Wildlife Trust as Marine Conservation Officer and Warden of the Purbeck Marine Wildlife Reserve for fourteen years and is currently Education Officer of the Marine Conservation Society. She has spent many years exploring Dorset's underwater habitats, as well as sailing, walking the coast and leading guided walks. She is also an Auxiliary Coastguard.

JIM WHITE graduated in Botany from London University, and his first post was with the Field Studies Council in Devon. He has since served as conservation officer of the Hampshire and Isle of Wight Trust and advised Hampshire County Council on conservation management. He has worked for English Nature since 1979, and is now team manager of their Dorset Office. He has a particular interest in habitat conservation and the smaller plants.

JOHN WRIGHT is a freshwater ecologist. After research in Canada on wetlands and at Reading University on chalk streams, he joined the Institute of Freshwater Ecology river laboratory near Wareham in 1977, where he specialises in river invertebrates. He is currently on the Conservation and Scientific Committee of the Dorset Wildlife Trust, and is Chairman of the Coombe Heath Nature Reserve Management Committee.

FRONT COVER *Spring flowers on chalk and limestone cliffs, St Oswald's Bay, Dorset.*

FOLLOWING PAGE *Pyramidal orchids on the Dorset Wildlife Trust Fontmell Down Nature Reserve.*

BACK COVER *A red squirrel; a puffin; hedge-laying at Kingcombe Meadows; bluebells, wild garlic, campion and yellow archangel; a small pearl bordered fritillary butterfly*

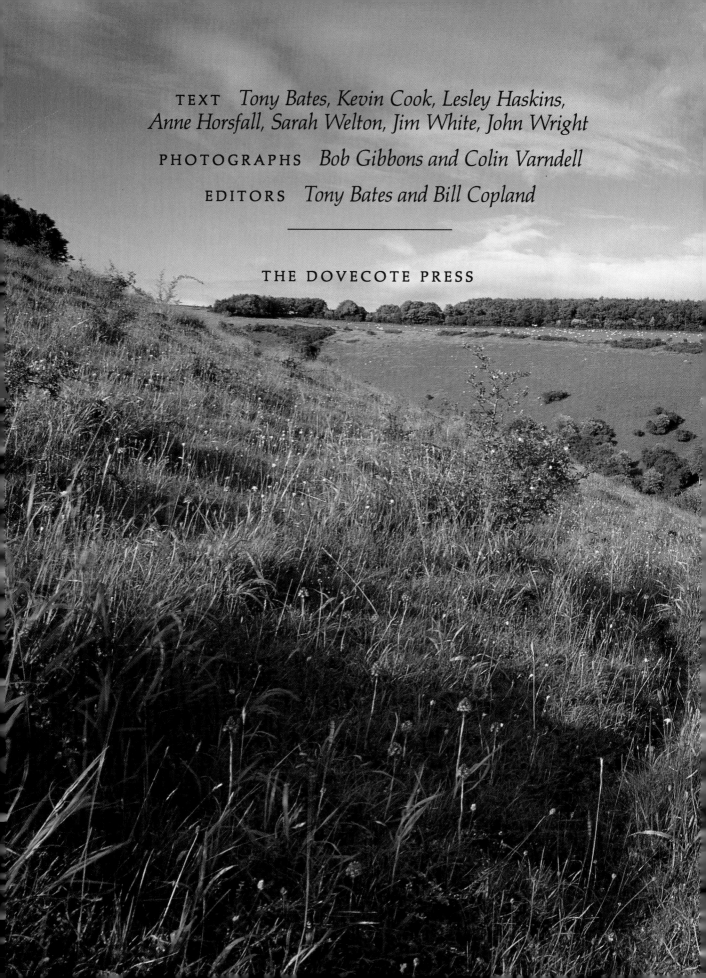

TEXT   *Tony Bates, Kevin Cook, Lesley Haskins, Anne Horsfall, Sarah Welton, Jim White, John Wright*

PHOTOGRAPHS   *Bob Gibbons and Colin Varndell*

EDITORS   *Tony Bates and Bill Copland*

THE DOVECOTE PRESS

The Natural History of
DORSET

THE DORSET WILDLIFE TRUST

Woodmice eating blackberries on the edge of a Dorset wood.

First published in 1997 by
The Dovecote Press Ltd
Stanbridge, Wimborne, Dorset BH21 4JD

Text: © The Dorset Wildlife Trust 1997
Photographs: © Tony Bates, Kevin Cook, Bob Gibbons,
Mike Lane, Peter Tinsley, Colin Varndell, Peter Wilson 1997

Typeset in Palatino by The Typesetting Bureau Ltd, Wimborne, Dorset
Printed and bound in Singapore

ISBN 1 874336 40 7 [paperback]
ISBN 1 874336 41 5 [hardback]

CONTENTS

ACKNOWLEDGEMENTS

THE TEXT

The idea of this book came from a small team from the Dorset Wildlife Trust. Its framework was then planned by Tony Bates, Kevin Cook, Bob Gibbons and Anne Horsfall. The Trust is immensely grateful to the authors, editors and photographers involved. All of them contributed a great deal of time and work, free of charge, in order that the Trust should benefit from the royalties and to enable the book's price to be kept as low as possible.

We are particularly grateful to Professor David Bellamy for the Foreword, and to Helen Brotherton for her introduction. In addition to the principal authors, we are also grateful to Dr Alan Grey for the section on Poole Harbour, Don Moxom for the section on the Fleet, and Christopher Welton for 'Moulding the Coastline' — all of which appear in the first chapter.

The authors and the Trust would also like to acknowledge the helpful advice given by the following: Sharon Abbott, Humphrey Bowen, Eileen Bowman, Robert Brunt, Paul Comer, Mike Cosgrove, Deborah Elton, Jane Franklin, Neil Gartshore, Maureen Keats, Mike Ladle, Colin Morris, David Pearman, Jeremy Powne, Richard Surry and Peter Tinsley.

The following must also be thanked: Caroline Pollard (BP); Mark Holloway (Bournemouth Borough Council); Chris Parker (British Herpetological Society); Martin Warren (Butterfly Conservation); Andy Nicholson, Tim Brody-James, Ian Nicholls, Nick Squirrel, Doug Kite (English Nature); Richard Burden, Phil Stirling, Hamish Murray, Terry Sweeney, Andy Elliott (Dorset County Council); Alison Stewart, Bryan Edwards (Dorset Environmental Records Centre); East Dorset District Council; Judith Crompton (Environment Agency); Major Mick Burgess (MoD Ranges Officer); Julian Homer, William Keighley (National Trust); Jez Martin (Poole Borough Council); Brian Pickess, Martin Slater, Nigel Symes (Royal Society for the Protection of Birds); Nick Collinson (Woodland Trust). The chapter on the Heaths is dedicated to the Institute of Terrestrial Ecology, Furzebrook, and those who work there.

THE PHOTOGRAPHS

The Dorset Wildlife Trust and the Dovecote Press would like to thank the following photographers for their generosity in providing the photographs for this book. Their support has helped fill page after page with a whole range of quite remarkable photographs, many of which have never been published before.

Tony Bates: frontispiece, 10, 26, 32, 36/37, 38 (left), 44/45, 48 (bottom), 57 (top), 80, 82, 88/89, 91 (top), 101 (top & bottom), 133 (top), 137 (bottom), 139 (top), 145, 147 (top & bottom).

Kevin Cook: 34, 35.

Bob Gibbons: front cover, 12/13, 15, 17 (top left, top right, bottom), 20, 21, 22 (top), 23 (top), 24 (top & bottom), 25 (middle & bottom), 31, 33, 39, 40 (left), 42 (left), 47, 48 (top), 49, 50 (top & bottom), 51 (top & bottom), 52, 53, 54 (left & right), 55 (left & right), 57 (bottom), 63, 65, 66/67, 71, 73 (top), 78 (left & right), 79, 81, 83, 85 (left & right), 93, 94, 98 (bottom), 99, 102, 112/113, 115, 117, 118, 120, 121, 122, 127 (top), 128, 129, 130/131, 132 (top & bottom), 133 (bottom), 135 (bottom), 140/141, 148 (top), 149, 152 (top), 153.

Mike Lane: 60 (right), 87 (top), 108 (top left), 126 (right), 127 (bottom).

Natural Image: 60 (top), 105.

Peter Tinsley: 40 (right), 41, 42 (right), 43.

Colin Varndell: 4, 11 (top & bottom), 14, 18 (top & bottom), 19, 22 (bottom), 23 (bottom), 25 (top), 27, 28, 29, 30, 38 (right), 58, 59, 60 (left), 68, 70 (bottom left & bottom right), 73 (bottom), 74, 87 (bottom) 91 (bottom), 92, 95, 97, 98 (top), 100, 103, 104, 106, 107 (bottom left & bottom right), 108 (top right & bottom), 109, 110, 111, 116, 119, 123 (top & bottom), 124, 125 (top), 134, 135 (top), 136, 138, 139 (bottom), 142, 148 (bottom), 150, 155, 156.

Peter Wilson: 56 (top & bottom), 70 (top left & top right), 75, 86 (top & bottom), 107 (top), 125 (bottom), 126 (left), 152 (bottom).

FOREWORD

BY PROFESSOR DAVID BELLAMY OBE
PRESIDENT, THE WILDLIFE TRUSTS

Dorset may no longer be 'Far from the Madding Crowd' but it still boasts a wealth of wildlife, as you will realize when you read this book.

Thanks to the people of this fair county, and especially its Wildlife Trust, over eighty nature reserves are now protected and in good heart. As an oasis often surrounded by a sea of destructive change, each is a genetic bank ready to support a sustainable future.

Along with the other Wildlife Trusts across Britain, the Dorset Wildlife Trust is working with government agencies, business, land-owners and farmers, local organizations and schools to reverse the impoverishment of the environment which has been so evident in recent years, and to recreate the former richness and variety in landscapes and wildlife – making it a saner, safer place in which ordinary people can bring up their families and watch the intricate beauty of nature reflected in the passing seasons.

I hope you enjoy this book. Give it pride of place in your library, and give your county, be it Dorset or any other, pride of place in your hearts. Redouble your efforts to work with your local Trust or any other body which is heaven-bent on saving the natural world on which we all depend.

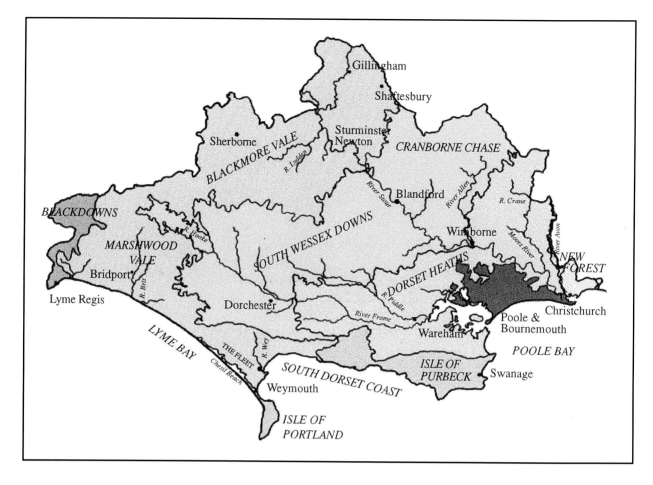

INTRODUCING DORSET

This is a book about the wild plants and animals of Dorset. This small county in southern England is much loved for the character and scenic beauty of its coast and countryside. The Dorset environment, largely rural, still attractive, displays great variety within a relatively small compass. Variety is literally the spice of life when it comes to natural history and nowhere is more varied for its size. The landscapes reflect the underlying geology. The rocks determine the nature of the soils and the soils often decide what use man has put the land to. Thus, both rocks and soil together, with climate and geographical distribution, create the habitats in which distinctive communities of plants and animals live.

The rock strata which underlie eastern England converge within Dorset and outcrop along its coast, giving great variety to the scenery and much attraction for geologists. A natural history book is not the place for a detailed geological account, but the first chapter does describe how the dramatic landscape of the coast has evolved from the range of outcropping rock formations.

Five broad divisions based on geological characteristics make up the county. They are the Isle of Purbeck, with its limestone plateau, clay vale and chalk ridge; the broad Tertiary rocks, sands and gravels which underlie the heathland landscape of south-east Dorset; the rolling downland underlain by chalk, stretching in a wide sweep across the centre of the county and ending in a steep escarpment at the northern edge; the heavy clays of the Blackmore Vale bounded by limestone hills to the north-west; and the complex limestone and sandstone hills divided by clay vales in the west, such as the Marshwood Vale.

DORSET PAST & PRESENT

BY HELEN BROTHERTON CBE
PRESIDENT, THE DORSET WILDLIFE TRUST

*Helen Brotherton has lived in Dorset for over half a century.
For the last 35 years she has been the inspiration of the Dorset Wildlife Trust,
serving successively as Secretary, Chairman and currently President. In spite of
the administrative load involved in advancing the Trust's work she has remained
a knowledgeable field naturalist and enthusiastic lover of wild plants and
animals. There is no-one more appropriate to introduce this new book on the
natural history of the county she loves best.*

I was reluctant to leave my friends and favourite natural history places when I moved to Dorset in 1946. However, Dorset instantly captivated me and I enjoyed the freedom of carefree exploration with little thought of the environmental threats to come.

We lived in Canford Cliffs, where the large gardens and open spaces had been neglected during the war and simply teemed with wildlife. Almost every heather clump had its sand lizards, creatures that were new to me. I found my first smooth snake and had glow worms lighting my path to the sea. War-time shore defences had created shallow tidal lagoons attracting grebes and divers. I could hardly believe my eyes one spring when a couple of ravens and a peregrine falcon had a mock battle above our local cliff. Rabbits, rats and woodmice were too abundant, but I managed to tolerate squirrel intrusions at my bird-table as the squirrels then were red! At first I knew of only one pair of urban foxes, but they steadily increased with the consequent disappearance of the rats and rabbits. Sparrowhawks nested successfully in the well-wooded Canford Cliffs and Branksome Park at a time when, as it later transpired, persistent agricultural chemicals were preventing young being hatched over much of the British countryside.

Studland Heath and the Sandbanks-Shell Bay Ferry were to remain closed for the next two years while explosives were cleared, and the area remained thoroughly remote. I was enchanted to see an otter amusing itself jumping on and off a barrel buoy at Poole Harbour entrance! Later, when Studland Heath and Harbour shores could be explored, otter traces were everywhere. Where the vast Sandbanks Car Park now is there were still sand dunes and, in winter, a merlin was often hunting there. Purple sandpipers could be seen feeding on the rocks by the Ferry.

Petrol was short, traffic was light, so bicycling was a pleasure. Signposts, removed during the war, took a long time to return to the lanes, and I well remember my disappointment when I couldn't relocate a remote area of heath where I had previously found a pair of Montague's Harriers. It is difficult now to appreciate how few people were around then. When I first came to

Storm clouds over Brownsea Island, which Helen Brotherton helped the National Trust and Dorset Wildlife Trust to acquire in 1962.

Dorset one could sometimes walk from Shell Bay to Swanage, or spend a whole day on the Arne peninsula, without meeting a soul. Birdwatchers were so rare that if you met someone using field glasses you spoke to them and exchanged news. The County Bird Report editor, wishing to form the Dorset Field Ornithology Group to help him with his task, could find only fifteen other experienced bird watchers!

In Dorset it was these ornithologists who first recognised the habitat destruction arising mostly from agricultural change propelled by the apparent need to grow more and more food in the post-war years. Downland became arable overnight. One country doctor, used to having a picnic lunch in the course of his rounds, found his favourite spot had become a tiny island in an arable sea where once flower-rich slopes of permanent grass had stretched far into the distance. Practices such as stubble burning were shown by the Game Conservancy to be adversely affecting partridges. The otter population was wiped out by river pollution. Birds of prey being at the top of the food chain accumulated persistent toxic chemicals in lethal doses. With huge faster-moving tractors no driver could be expected to see and move stone curlew or lapwing

eggs where once they would have been rescued. Extensive drainage schemes did away with traditional nesting sites for snipe, curlew and redshank. Heathlands were afforested with conifers; Winfrith Heath was chosen for the Atomic Energy Establishment to avoid the use of good agricultural land. Poole and Bournemouth began to expand across the heaths. Even in Canford Cliffs the large gardens vanished under blocks of flats. Public open spaces were tidied up and features such as one untidy hedge in Poole Park where I had found harvest mouse nests suddenly vanished. Dorset wildlife, which had enjoyed a good wartime, was under post-war siege.

In the environmentally unfriendly 1950s and 60s conservationists were few and far between. The Dorset Wildlife Trust, originally named the Dorset Naturalists' Trust, was formed in 1961. It had to blaze a trail and its pioneers became resigned to being thought eccentric, to say the least! Help however, was at hand. The Nature Conservancy (now English Nature) established a research station and conservation centre at Furzebrook near Wareham. We were delighted to find a distinguished scientist and outstanding field naturalist in charge, Dr. (now Professor) Norman Moore. The long-established Dorset Natural

History and Archaeological Society supported the Trust. The National Trust was acquiring coast and countryside of great wildlife value and the Royal Society for the Protection of Birds was also seeking nature reserves in Dorset. A spirit of co-operation between official and voluntary organisations quickly grew and added strength to face the urgent challenges of the times. Nature conservation began to change from a hobby for the few to a concern of the many.

While many battles for nature were fought in public inquiries and elsewhere and losses continued to be sustained, there was a gradual change of attitude among those who, privately, or as decision-makers in public bodies, controlled the fate of the land. The need to maintain a healthy environment with a rich and varied wildlife began to be recognised. For example, although the Trust enjoyed the help and co-operation of the Forestry Commission from the start, they were required to concentrate on timber production alone. Now landscape, wildlife and public enjoyment are foremost, allowing some areas within the forests to be returned to heathland. Farmers in Dorset have always been sympathetic to conservation as individuals but now the whole grant-aiding scheme has changed and farming for wildlife is widely practised. Then look how much attention is now paid by large companies like British Petroleum to protect sensitive areas and to minimise the impact of major enterprises like the extraction of oil from Poole Bay and Harbour. The sky has indeed brightened over the last thirty years.

Lest this should seem complacent I must finish with a warning. Although there is a much better climate of opinion and our local teachers should be thanked for their efforts with young people, problems remain and vigilance is essential. Housing development continues apace and further expansion of gravel-winning poses severe threats. Once familiar species remain uncommon. Corn buntings have disappeared from most of their former haunts and yellowhammers are no longer found in every stretch of hedgerow. Changes continue — some for good like the return of

One of Dorset's rarest birds, now beginning to make a comeback. A young peregrine on the cliffs near West Bay.

The intimate west Dorset landscape, seen here at Burcombe, near Poorton.

cowslips on by-passes — many for ill. Past experience shows that new and unexpected threats are liable to turn up overnight. The most important thing, however, is the will to protect and manage our environment beneficially. Dorset is the envy of many visitors; we who live here are lucky; please play your part in protecting the plants and animals you will meet in the pages of this book. I hope you enjoy reading it.

THE COAST

MOULDING THE COASTLINE

The Dorset coast is internationally famous for its spectacular landscape and scenery. Features such as Durdle Door and Old Harry are familiar from postcards and calendars the world over. To seek the reasons, and the stunning variety of habitats and species to be found on the Dorset coast, we need to cast our minds back millions of years and look at the rocks underlying and outcropping at the coast, as well as the dramatic changes which have affected them over a time-scale we can barely comprehend.

The geological succession exposed at the coast shows a wide variety of different types of sedimentary sequences, which in turn are representative of nearly all the rocks in eastern England. These were laid down as sediments under varying shallow sea and freshwater conditions. In due course they were subjected to massive pressures, similar to those forming the Alps, leading to the formation of the coastline we know today. Because all these rock types are so well represented over such a short length of coast, Dorset attracts geologists from all over the world. What is so exciting is that the county's geology is not just a study of the past; change is still happening. The Dorset coastline is an active system, which is constantly being tempered by the processes of wind, rain and sea. We can see examples of erosion and deposition at every turn during a walk along the coast path.

The Dorset coast at Durdle Door with drifts of horseshoe vetch in the foreground.

The oldest rocks forming the Dorset coast come from the Triassic period of around 220 million years ago. This is best seen in the Lyme Regis area, a famous locality for fossil collecting. Here the coastline is dominated by muddy cliffs, which are variable in height and prone to landslips. Mudslides are common, extending from the cliffs across the short beach and into the sea. The taller cliffs near Lyme Regis are supported by layers of sandstone, giving the soft rock some support.

The rocks of the Jurassic period (213-144 million years ago) are characterised by clays and shales, which are soft and easily eroded, supported by layers of more resistant limestone, oolite and sandstone. This combination of hard and soft layers caused the formation of the rock ledges which are such a dominant feature of the Dorset coastline, forming a distinct habitat for marine life. This is best shown at Kimmeridge Bay, where the oil shales contain layers of harder limestone. Above these clay-rich rocks are the world famous Portland stone beds. These massive limestones are widely used as a building stone due to their strength; it is this which has resulted in the dramatic, tall buttressed cliffs of Gad Cliff, west of Kimmeridge Bay and St. Aldhelm's Head, both notable bird nesting sites. As the name suggests, we have Portland stone to thank for the rugged Isle of Portland.

Looking west towards Lyme Regis from the Spittles, where the blue lias and sandstone cliffs are prone to landslips.

ABOVE *Looking west from St Oswald's Bay. Much of the Dorset coast is being considered as a World Heritage Site on the strength of its geological importance, an honour only so far accorded to such sites as the Grand Canyon.*

BELOW *Simplified geological map of Dorset.*

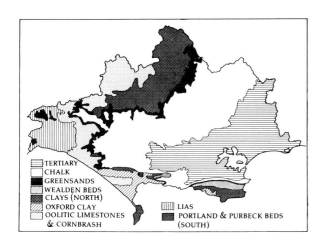

TERTIARY
CHALK
GREENSANDS
WEALDEN BEDS
CLAYS (NORTH)
OXFORD CLAY
OOLITIC LIMESTONES
& CORNBRASH
LIAS
PORTLAND & PURBECK BEDS
(SOUTH)

The Cretaceous rocks, which sit above the Portland beds, date from 144 to 65 million years ago. They start with the Purbeck limestones, which are overlain by the soft and easily eroded Wealden beds. The Cretaceous sequence is mostly represented by the Chalk. This is the thickest bed of the region and therefore influences a large proportion of the coast, forming the distinctive high white cliffs and features such as the Old Harry rocks.

The youngest rocks are those of the Tertiary (65 to 2 million years ago). These occur on the eastern section of the coast and are composed of sands, gravels and clays. The clays form the basis of the pottery industry in the Poole area, whilst we owe Bournemouth's wide beaches and the development of the dune systems at Studland and Shell Bay to the sands.

The most important event in shaping the Dorset coast took place about 25 million years ago. It was then that the movement of the earth's landmasses caused Africa to collide with Europe, creating immense pressures which thrust up the major European mountain belts. The south coast of England was subjected to much slighter pressure which, even so, took horizontally lying beds of rock and turned them on their sides. In some places the pressure was sufficient to turn the rocks almost entirely upside down.

Gradually the forces of nature started to erode the rocks to form the unique coastline of today. Lulworth Cove, for example, was formed by erosion after the sea had broken through the resistant barrier of Portland limestone, washing away the soft sands of the Wealden beds behind, before once again being slowed by the tall chalk cliffs. Continued erosion will lead to a more developed cove with a wider mouth to the open sea, which will eventually be completely broken down to form the shape of the coastline seen at Worbarrow Bay, where the sea has eroded the softer rocks almost entirely back to the chalk.

We must not forget, either, that the 'landscape' and scenery beneath the waves is as varied and dramatic as that above. The seabed is not a desert. There are plains and ridges, rocky reefs and ledges – you only need to look at an Admiralty chart or take an echo sounding to see for yourself. Even the remains of eroded cliffs form underwater reefs. Much of what we have recently discovered about the rock formations and features under the sea off Dorset is the result of oil exploration, which in turn has occurred because of the oil-bearing rocks deep beneath the seabed.

It is this rich variety of sedimentary rock types and the soils derived from them that makes Dorset's coast so spectacular. Without the ever-changing shape of the coastline and the conditions affecting it – wind, water, frost and changing seasons – we would not have the varied habitats and fascinating coastal and marine wildlife, nor indeed the impressive landscapes illustrated in this book.

WILDLIFE HABITATS

The present coastline of our county, with its headlands, bays and beaches, is relatively recent, created by relentless post-glacial erosion and rising sea levels from about 18,000 years ago. Then the Dorset shore-line was some 150 metres lower and several kilometres further south than it is today. The coastal rocks and soils are of sedimentary origin and are often rich in fossils – ranging from the older, triassic lias at Lyme Regis to the younger, tertiary sands of the Poole Basin. Between these extremes are fine examples of geological formations, some known internationally from their Dorset localities: Bridport sands, Kimmeridge clay, Portland and Purbeck beds.

This diversity in rock formations provides a wide range of wildlife habitats: chalk cliffs from White Nothe to Lulworth Cove and again at Worbarrow Bay and Ballard Down; limestones at Portland and in Purbeck; other cliffs of lias, clay, shale or greensand. Then there are unstable undercliffs with landslips or mudflows, beaches with sand, shingle or dunes, inlets and harbours with mud flats, marshes and reed beds. Every part of the coast is at the mercy of the weather and the ceaseless motion of the sea. Most exposed cliffs clearly show stratification, with ledges and outcrops where soft sediments have weathered more rapidly than harder rocks. We will now see how this diversity along our coastline influences wildlife.

CLIFFS AND QUARRIES

Cliffs are habitats for many maritime plants. Wherever there are ledges, crevices and gullies, any plant able to tolerate exposure to wind and salt spray will take hold. Sea campion, sea mayweed, sea pink or thrift, red valerian and various grasses are widely established. More specialised and often succulent plants grow on the coastal limestones, notably golden samphire, rock samphire, wild cabbage, Danish scurvygrass, sea aster, and species of rock sea-lavender.

Limestone has been quarried in Portland and

ABOVE *Rock samphire, a succulent whose tiny summer-flowering yellowish-green flowers develop into purple-green fruits.*

RIGHT *Wild or sea cabbage, from which the cultivated cabbage originated.*

BELOW RIGHT *Red valerian in flower at Church Ope Cove, Portland.*

Purbeck for centuries. Man-made caves, fallen rocks and quarry spoil are now exceptional wildlife habitats. Stony places give cover for rabbits and other mammals, and may conceal adders and common lizards. Eleven of the fourteen British bats have been recorded along the Dorset coast and several of the old Purbeck quarries are used as winter roosts.

Wild flowers are especially plentiful on Portland. At Church Ope Cove there are rock stonecrop, hairy-fruited corn salad, rue-leaved saxifrage, hoary stock, and ivy broomrape. Portland also has uncommon ferns and grasses, notably sea spleenwort, western polypody and maidenhair fern, sea hard-grass and fern-grass. Brambles are commonplace, often with areas of well-established buddleia, cotoneaster, tree mallow and wild privet, all important food plants for insects. Many lichens and several rare mosses occur on the hard limestones and calcareous soils of the Portland peninsula.

The marine lichens are clearly zoned: a lower black zone including *Lichina confinis* and *Verrucaria maura* among the limpets; a yellow zone with *Caloplaca marina* and *Caloplaca thallincola*; and a well-represented upper grey zone which also includes the rare *Rocella phycopsis*, known in the area for nearly two hundred years, and several uncommon bryophytes on sheltered boulders.

Portland is also renowned for its insects, many of which are nationally rare or endangered. Disused quarries, where there is plenty of horseshoe-vetch and other legumes, are colonised by a unique form of the silver-studded blue butterfly, a species more usually found on heathland. Moths include the bordered gothic, the four-spotted and the Portland ribbon wave which live in rough grassland by the cliffs, and two very rare tineid moths, one found only among boulders and scree on Portland and near Swanage. Other scarce insects in various other sites include species of cranefly, chafer beetle, ant and solitary wasp.

Common birds of the Dorset cliffs are feral pigeons, stock doves, starlings, jackdaws, swifts and rock pipits. Kestrels wheel high overhead, taking advantage of the constant updrafts before hovering over their prey. There is a long tradition of bird observation along the coast. Several hundred species have been recorded at Durlston, near Swanage, and there has been daily monitoring at the Portland Bird Observatory since 1961.

Rare or threatened species such as raven, peregrine and little tern continue to be closely observed at their nesting sites. Other birds are monitored regularly at selected sites and incoming migrants are ringed in several coastal localities. Of special interest are the nesting birds on the less accessible parts of the Purbeck cliffs between St.

Aldhelm's Head and Durlston. Here, Bird Hole, Bird Cove and Bird Rock are ancient landmarks. The limestone ledges have long been colonised by a succession of sea-birds from early spring. Successful rearing of young birds depends on lack of disturbance, but may also be affected by pollution and food supply in the open sea.

The numbers of auks have declined. There are fewer puffins and razorbills, but rather more guillemots, including the attractive bridled form. Puffins were once common, hiding their eggs in recesses deep inside the 'puffin ledge' along the cliff face, but they may no longer lay there. Breeding kittiwakes and fulmars seem to be increasing. Herring gulls are common but greater blackbacked gulls less so. Nesting shags are numerous, whilst cormorants prefer to nest further away at White Nothe, Gad Cliff near Tyneham and on chalk cliffs below Ballard Down. Both ravens and peregrine falcons have survived persecution and the consequences of pesticides to nest again in small numbers on Purbeck cliffs.

OPPOSITE TOP *Puffins have declined on the Dorset coast, but can still be spotted on the less accessible limestone ledges of the Purbeck cliffs.*

LEFT *A fulmar near Dancing Ledge.*

RIGHT *A razorbill. Like all auks, razorbills are good divers and underwater swimmers. They lay only one egg, usually among boulders on cliff ledges.*

Early spider orchids on the Purbeck coast.

CLIFF-TOPS

Dorset cliff-tops are fragile habitats, vulnerable to landslips and erosion, and affected by frost in winter and drought in summer. Footpaths may be worn to bedrock, or become crevices in soft clay soils and constantly need to be re-aligned as sections fall away. Gorse, brambles, blackthorn and other vegetation help stabilise cliff edges and dense bushes provide nesting sites for stonechats and meadow pipits. Warm south-facing slopes and screes may be refuges for adders, lizards, slow-worms and the insects they feed on, attracting kestrel, merlin, little owl and other birds of prey.

Several distinctive plants of limestone and chalk occur on cliff-top grassland, especially in Purbeck. They include the early spider orchid, the endemic early gentian and nit-grass, rare plants but sometimes numerous in a few places. In taller grassland, often with tor grass and soft brome, are Scotch thistle, slender thistle and milk thistle, white horehound and Nottingham catchfly, all favoured by a variety of insects. Carrot broom-rape is sometimes a parasite on wild carrot and houndstongue occurs sporadically. These sub-maritime plants are able to grow inland but take advantage of the milder coastal climate and the warmer, well drained soils. Several small ephemerals such as whitlow-grass, cornsalad and early forget-me-not come into flower before the winter moisture dries up. Some cliff-top plants are relics of former cultivation. Black mustard is widespread but pheasant's-eye, corn buttercup, shepherd's needle and slender hare's-ear are rare. Corn parsley, hairy buttercup and small-flowered buttercup are locally plentiful. An unusual rarity on cliff-top edges above West Bay is the aptly named stinking goosefoot, growing in eroded sandstone around rabbit burrows. Other occasional relics of the past are the poisonous henbane and the opium poppy.

UNDERCLIFFS

In many ways, the undercliffs are the most unusual of all the habitats to be found along the coast. They have formed from landslips, often where unstable cliffs have sheared, slumped and slid over wet surfaces of impervious clays, creating screes, broken terraces, deep crevices, mud flows, and jumbles of rocks. Dense vegetation covers the older landslips and gradually becomes established on freshly exposed areas.

Most undercliffs are well-known, at least by name. East of Lyme Regis are the Spittles and Black Ven, spilling into Lyme Bay. Next is Cain's Folly near Charmouth and the Wear Cliffs under Golden Cap. On Portland are the rocky east and west Weares. The terraced undercliffs extending below White Nothe are now a nature reserve. The most familiar landslips in Purbeck are at Flower's Barrow, Gad Cliff, Houns tout, Chapman's Pool, Durlston Bay and below Ballard Down. None of these undercliffs are on the scale of the famous 8-mile landslip from Axmouth in Devon to Lyme

Regis on the Dorset border, but each is a small wilderness area for wildlife.

Many different kinds of plants are to be found. Rare lichens occur below St Aldhelm's Head and on the hard chalk under Ballard Cliff. The first flowering plant to colonise new mud flows is coltsfoot and in the Black Ven area its leaves are host to the larva of a rare gelechiid moth. In seepages and standing water, common reed, various rushes, horsetails, common fleabane and less usual marsh plants such as brookweed, marsh helleborine and the southern marsh orchid are locally common. Often there are clumps of stinking iris, and in western undercliffs its large pods provide food for the rare iris weevil.

In drier places, viper's bugloss and red valerian are conspicuous among many other common plants. More locally there is Portland spurge, not confined to Portland, great lettuce, bithynian and other vetches, and under Thorncombe Beacon, the rare white flowered slender centaury. The older, more stable, parts of undercliffs have extensive areas of dense, often impenetrable thickets where bushes of blackthorn, bramble, wild rose, gorse, privet, also coarse grasses and wild madder grow unchecked. The thickets are natural sanctuaries for small numbers of roe deer, foxes, hares, rabbits, badgers, as well as many birds, reptiles, insects

The terraced undercliffs below White Nothe. The dense thickets and scrub of Dorset's undercliffs form one of its rarest habitats, rich in flowers, insects, birds and reptiles. They also provide sanctuary for small numbers of roe deer, badgers and hares.

and other creatures. Natural regeneration of ash and sycamore among the shrubs indicate the beginnings of woodland.

Coastal inlets and the Purbeck 'gwyles' of Tyneham, Encombe, Chapman's Pool and Winspit are also places of scrub, thickets, grassy slopes and small streams. Sheltered valleys and undercliffs are ideal landfall for many summer migrant birds, including nightingales and warblers, as well as hundreds of moths and butterflies, such as red admiral, clouded yellow and painted lady.

The variety of habitat ensures that insects are especially abundant. From Lyme Regis to Eype are sites of national and even international importance for scarce species, notably beetles, bees and wasps. These include spider-hunting wasps, digger wasps, halictid bees, an andrenid bee, a megachilid bee and different kinds of rare beetles.

Mating clouded yellow butterflies. This species arrives in Dorset from southern Europe, breeding here in warmer summers.

A Lulworth skipper, one of Dorset's distinctive coastal butterflies.

Then there are other rarities: Morris' wainscot moth on tall fescue; Cepero's groundhopper; rufous grasshopper; the wood-white butterfly, perhaps a local migrant from the Devon undercliffs. Other invertebrates, nationally important because of their scarcity, are found in a variety of places almost exclusively along the Purbeck coast, including undercliffs. Most famous is the Lulworth skipper butterfly in rough grassland where tor-grass is the larval food-plant, and several moths with exotic names: beautiful gothic, chalk carpet, crescent dart, Kent black arches, and some small moths found only in Purbeck. Other specialities include Lesne's earwig, several parasitic and ground bees, and two rare grassland spiders.

THE COASTAL FRINGE

Characteristic plants grow along the edges of the coast above the beaches. One of many rich areas is the rough, unstable grassland between the sea and the dismantled Weymouth to Portland railway just north of Ferry Bridge. Here are rare legumes, the bithynian vetch, grass vetchling and yellow vetchling, and along the old line are both round-leaved crane's-bill, the related little robin, and many casual plants such as wall rocket, wild lettuce, fennel and purple toadflax.

Short turf in coastal areas is studded with small plants such as early forget-me-not, sea pearlwort, sea mouse-ear, several small clovers and medicks, sometimes sea storksbill, dwarf centaury and others able to withstand grazing rabbits and trampling by the many visitors to the seaside. Conspicuous alien plants now firmly established are hoary cress, which reached Britain in 1809, between Weymouth and Abbotsbury; Hottentot fig, especially around Portland and Poole Harbour; and more recently, piri-piri burr from the southern hemisphere in the Knoll Beach car park at Studland.

Several places are notable for rare plants. The stable sandy grassland between Portland Harbour and the sea is the site of the purple-flowered broomrape, and nearby is four-leaved allseed.

The rare bithynian vetch flowers between May and July and can be seen in the rough grassland near the old Weymouth to Portland railway near Ferry Bridge.

Purple broomrape near Ferry Bridge.

Dwarf mouse-ear chickweed is sometimes seen in Purbeck, and from Studland eastwards are a few sites for the dotted sedge, spring vetch, hairy bird's-foot trefoil and several small clovers as well as rare grasses, rough dog's-tail, hare's-tail, early meadow-grass, bulbous meadow-grass, Bermuda grass, and great brome.

Some plants long-established along the coast were once important for food or medicinal purposes and it is interesting to speculate on their origin. At Abbotsbury alone there is sea beet, sea-kale, sea-holly, leek, garlic, black mustard and wild celery. Some of the cliffs of Portland and Purbeck are covered in both rock and golden samphires, wild cabbage and Danish scurvygrass, and on the edge of the Fleet are occasional tall clumps of marsh-mallow. Many attractive insects benefit from the plentiful plant life and occur along most parts of the Dorset coast. There are the bloody-nosed beetles on grassland, both the grey and great green bush-crickets, coneheads, hover-flies in great numbers, the rose chafer, the sulphur beetle on carrot and other umbellifers, an iridescent green beetle on the many yellow composites, and the scarce lesser cockroach in bare areas.

A grey bush-cricket, another characteristic coastal species.

SHINGLE

The great bank of pebbles which form the Chesil Beach is probably the most well-known feature of the Dorset coast. It extends from West Bay near Bridport to Weymouth and links the Isle of Portland to the mainland. The massive eastern part encloses the shallow, brackish waters of the Fleet lagoon for eight miles from Abbotsbury to the narrow entrance at Ferry Bridge on Portland Harbour.

The south-facing slopes of the beach are exposed to wind and tide, forming a highly unstable

A drift of sea campion on the landward side of Chesil Beach, where it is sandier and more stable.

ABOVE *Sea kale.*

LEFT *The purple-blue blossoms of the July flowering sea pea.*

BELOW *The deep-rooted yellow-horned poppy.*

shingle bank. The pebbles are regularly shifted and graded with the largest deposited at the Portland end. One of its features on the landward side are the buttressed ravines formed when wave action forces sea water through the bank. The ridges are eventually colonised by sea campion and a succession of other plants. Notable species well-rooted among the pebbles of the beach are sea pea, yellow horned-poppy and sea kale. Sea kale became rare in Dorset when once it was collected for the London market, but now is locally common along the beach.

The vegetation changes near the Fleet where shrubby sea-blite is a conspicuous shrub along the brackish inner strandline, its stems yellow with the lichen *Xanthoria parietina*. Annual seablite also occurs here in damp, sandy spots, sometimes with sea heath, sea spurge and sea sandwort, and the attractive stiff saltmarsh grass on stable shingle.

Where the beach is sandier and more stable, the expanses of sea campion are joined by thrift, sea mayweed, yellow stonecrop, sea beet, orache, curled dock, woody nightshade, often with bristly ox-tongue and prickly sow-thistle. Rarities include sea-holly and sea bindweed, also found among the sand dunes of Studland Bay. The commonest grass is red fescue, often well-established and stabilizing the sand.

The Chesil Beach is an area famous for its invertebrate specialities. As well as very uncommon snails, spiders and insects which live in shingle and vegetated habitats, there are species of rare coastal bees and beetles – and the scaly cricket in its only British site.

SAND DUNES

The dune system of Studland Heath, also known as the South Haven Peninsula, is an area of many important wildlife habitats, much of it within a National Nature Reserve. This dry and windswept area was studied in detail by Capt. Cyril Diver, the first director-general of the Nature Conservancy, now English Nature, together with other naturalists in the 1930s. In three centuries dunes have developed from wind-blown sand deposited the length of Studland Bay, creating a series of ridges with damp hollows or 'slacks' between them. Gradually, a lagoon formed, and

■ *Older land of the peninsula* ▨ *Sand dunes*

Three maps showing the gradual formation of Little Sea, Studland, between 1721 and 1947. The promontory was once much narrower, and Little Sea was formed by two systems of sand dunes, one from the north, the other from the south, which finally met in the late 19th century, cutting off part of the bay and turning it into a freshwater lake.

A view of Little Sea.

A tufted duck on Radipole Lake Nature Reserve.

once cut off from the sea, developed into a fresh-water lake, Little Sea, in the south of the Reserve.

Studland Heath shows how plants can stabilise dunes. Above the strand, robust maritime grasses, sand couch, lyme grass and marram grass are among the first colonists, followed by sand sedge and dune fescue, sometimes with lichens, sea bindweed, sea holly, sea rocket and sea sandwort. A few unique insects, the sand dart moth and the shore wainscot moth, inhabit the foredunes, and older dunes are ideal habitats for butterflies, hoverflies, sand-wasps, ladybirds, horse-flies, other moths and snails. Specialities of the dunes are a rare damsel bug and a ground bug, and more moths, including the grass eggar, Portland moth and a scythridid moth found only at Studland.

As the sands gradually compact and stabilize, acidic dune grassland develops and many lichens become established, including at least fifteen species of *Cladonia* and a rather small number of flowering plants such as ragwort, centaury, yellow-wort and heath bedstraw. As humus slowly builds up among the dunes, scrub and open woodland with extensive gorse and heather, pine and sallow trees become established, whilst rushes, reeds and osmunda fern flourish in old bomb craters and other wet hollows.

MERES, MARSHES AND MUDFLATS

The Little Sea on Studland Heath, surrounded by expanses of reeds, bogbean and sallow is a year-round haven for numerous coastal and fresh-water birds. Another, much smaller lake in west Dorset is Burton Mere, lying behind the Chesil Beach near West Bexington. Burton Mere is enclosed by reeds and ditches and is a good site for flowers uncommon elsewhere, such as brookweed, amphibious bistort and narrow-leaved water-plantain, as well as nesting warblers, water vole, crested newt and many other aquatic creatures.

Other outstanding wetland sites for Dorset wildlife are the brackish waters of Radipole and Lodmoor near Weymouth, the Fleet, Poole Harbour with its mud-flats, salt marshes and reed-beds, and Christchurch Harbour including Hengistbury Head.

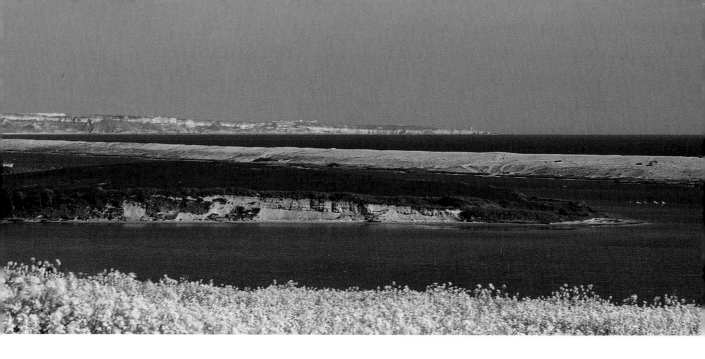

THE FLEET

The Fleet's evolution is recent in geological time, going back 18,000 years to the end of the last Ice Age when the sea level was 150 metres lower than it is today. As the ice melted and the sea levels rose, seawater flooded in behind the Chesil Beach from the eastern side of Portland. At first it was believed that the Fleet extended considerably to the west, shortening as the beach rolled back with the rising sea level: a conclusion drawn principally from the presence of fossil evidence, such as the lagoon cockle found in peat and clay deposits washed up on the beach after storms.

Today the Fleet stretches for 13 kilometres from Abbotsbury to Portland, and at high water covers an area of 4.9 sq. km. It maintains its only direct connection to Portland Harbour at Small Mouth, a strong tidal link that provides most of its seawater. It is also affected by the seawater continually percolating on a small scale through the Chesil Beach, and more dramatically during periodic storms when waves wash over and through the beach. No river serves the Fleet with freshwater, the sources of which are limited to numerous streams, trickles and run-offs along its landshore. Naturally there is a bias towards freshwater at the western end and, in winter, the

ABOVE *The Fleet and Chesil Beach from near Langton Herring, with Portland Bill just visible in the distance.*

OPPOSITE *A little tern holding a sand eel. Few birds choose a more hazardous nest-site. Following its arrival in the spring, the little tern nests close to the water's edge on bare shingle, making it easy prey for storms and foxes.*

increase in rainfall reduces its overall salinity. The Fleet's depth averages one metre, although the channels or lakes through which the tidal waters are distributed have been scoured out to 5 metres.

The water levels are, however, greatly affected by the weather, especially wind and air pressure. They are also subject to delays in the incoming tide due to the double low tide in Portland Harbour, the 'throttling' effect of the Narrows, the 70-100 metre channel that links Portland Harbour to the wider, shallower areas of the Fleet and a 'ponding-up' of water within the lagoon in the spring tides' cycle. The constriction of the water in the Narrows produces a current of up to six knots at flood and ebb tides. The effect on the seabed is predictable, transporting all but the more robust sediments further into the Fleet or out into Portland Harbour, leaving a seabed of bars of firmly packed pebbles and rock.

The marine flora and fauna that exist in the Fleet provide one of the most colourful British underwater scenes. As might be expected, they consist mainly of 'rapids-system' specialists, creatures capable of clinging to the substrate in these tide-swept conditions. These are encrusting and 'turf' seaweeds and an incredibly high population of anemones, sponges and sea squirts. Along the landshore where the water slackens, there are thick stands of seaweeds such as the bootlace weed and the alien Japanese seaweed, whilst opposite, under the Chesil, a combination of percolating seawater and static shingle has created unusual micro-habitats occupied by some rare invertebrates including tiny, specialised molluscs living in the spaces between the pebbles.

At the west end of the Narrows, the lagoon broadens and the water becomes shallower. Soft beds of organic mud cover this area and these beds contain important, extensive populations of two species of eel grass, two species of tassel weed and the rare foxtail stonewort. In addition, numerous filamentous green seaweeds grow in the summer, forming impassable rafts. A variety of invertebrate species exploit this verdant growth, including some distinct and highly unusual populations of molluscs. Most species are of an estuarine or truly lagoonal nature and a number are nationally very rare. How they survive in the supersaline conditions produced by high temperature water in the summer (up to 30 degrees centigrade), and in colder than normal sea temperatures in the winter, is something that has been intriguing scientists for a number of years.

The Fleet attracts a number of visiting species. Little terns breed on the Chesil, and numerous species of waders and other birds arrive in the spring and summer, including the little egret, a recent arrival which can be seen at the water's edge. At the same time shoals of fish such as sand smelt, bass and mullet arrive to feed on the abundant food thriving in the warm water. Perhaps the most spectacular scene is the arrival of the wildfowl in the autumn. Over 10,000 birds of the principal species – Brent goose, wigeon and coot – can be seen feasting upon the eel grass, along with 1,000 or more resident and visiting mute swans. Smaller numbers of pochard, tufted duck and scaup exploit the molluscs whilst sea ducks, such as red-breasted mergansers and goldeneye, chase three-spined sticklebacks and a species of prawn known locally as 'billy winters'.

The status of the Fleet for nature conservation is exceptionally high and it is protected as an internationally valued wetland, but its real custodian are the Ilchester Estate, who have owned the seabed and managed the area for many centuries.

ABOVE   *Studland Heath and Poole Harbour from Godlingston, with Brownsea Island shrouded in early-morning mist in the background.*

OPPOSITE PAGE   *High tide in Poole Harbour at Arne. Despite the shipping and pleasure craft in the busy main channels, much of the Harbour is made up of salt-marshes and quiet inlets and creeks.*

POOLE HARBOUR

At the highest spring tides the waters of Poole Harbour cover an area of more than 3,500 hectares. This vast natural harbour was about 1,000 hectares larger 6,000 years ago when the post-Glacial rise in sea level was at its highest. The retreat of the sea from this ancient shoreline, traceable today by a low bluff or by cliffs surrounding much of the Harbour, and the growth of sandspits at the mouth, has left behind a sheltered, highly-indented shoreline (more than 100 kms long) and the Harbour's picturesque wooded islands.

When the tide is at its lowest, it reveals a fascinating world of saltmarshes, glistening mudflats and shingle and sandy beaches. Although the difference between the highest and lowest tides of the year is less than two metres, the intertidal area comprises about 80% of the total. The Harbour is drained at low water by a relatively stable system of creeks (locally, and somewhat perversely, called 'lakes') and channels, which are pretty much the same as when they were first surveyed 200 years ago. Their movement is constrained by the many promontories and islands, and ultimately by the low-lying, sandy spits of Studland and Sandbanks which guard the entrance.

The small tidal range, and the fact that for two-thirds of the time water levels are above the mid-tide level, is an important feature of Poole Harbour, providing not only a sheltered environment for the growth of saltmarshes but ideal conditions for the development of the port of Poole. Indeed, the contrast which often strikes the newcomer is that between the bustling port and expanding holiday area on the north shore and the quiet bays and inlets along the southern edge — a contrast which is increasingly difficult to preserve.

The shoreline presents us with a rich variety of habitats, ranging from reed and marsh-covered mudflats to sandflats and shingle beaches. There are many interesting transitionary habitats where the saltmarshes adjoin valley mires, heathland, grazing marsh and water meadows. Reedbeds in particular are valued places for breeding birds. If we include the dunes and chalk cliffs near the Harbour mouth, most types of British coastal habitat are represented within a relatively small area. The beaches and flats range from glutinous muds to wave-rippled sand and firm shingle. Many of the shingle beaches are created from nearby eroding cliffs, the sea redistributing the pebbles derived from the Bagshot Beds and the Pleistocene gravels which cap them. Such cliffs, which tend to occur in the south and west of shores and islands, have built features such as the lagoon on Brownsea Island and the saltmarsh on north-west Furzey.

As might be expected, the richness of the habitats is matched by the flora and fauna. Arguably the most noticeable are the birds, different groups of which utilise the Harbour at different seasons. The busiest time of all is the winter, when thousands of shore-birds such as dunlin and redshank flock to feed on the intertidal flats, waterfowl such as wigeon and Brent geese feed on the adjoining fields, and diving birds such as grebes and mergansers fish the waters. Many species have a favourite part: the black-tailed godwit is mostly found in the muddy bays of Brands Bay, Newton Bay and Holes Bay, whilst its cousin, the bar-tailed godwit, prefers the sandy northern shore along Parkstone Bay. These preferences reflect the distribution of their favoured foods – the different species of benthic invertebrates in mudflats exposed at low tide. The shelduck, which occurs all the year round and nests around the Harbour, also likes the muddier areas. Other year-round residents include black-headed gulls, which nest in vast numbers on islands of saltmarsh near Holton Heath, and grey herons, which nest on Brownsea Island.

The fringing marshes are often rich in plant species, with drifts of sea lavender and sea pink

Sea lavender and Spartina *grass on the saltmarshes beside Poole Harbour.*

interspersed with the pale grey foliage of sea purslane being a memorable feature of the higher levels. Transitions to fresh water often carry sea club-rush, spike-rush, distant sedge, divided sedge, sea rush, saltmarsh rush, and grey club-rush, and on shingle beaches at higher levels the green and scarlet sea beet and shrubby sea-blite add a splash of colour.

In many ways the most interesting plant of the Poole Harbour saltmarshes is *Spartina* grass. The arrival, spread and subsequent decline of this sturdy plant has been the major force for change in the intertidal zone. First recorded from Ower in around 1890, *Spartina* had spread to cover more than 775 hectares (an area equivalent to 1,100 football pitches!) of mudflat by the time of the first aerial survey in 1924. In some areas of the upper Harbour, such as Keysworth, it trapped fine sediments to a depth of almost two metres and had a major impact on the distribution and depth of intertidal channels. Poole also played a significant part in the history of the grass, which was exported to stabilise mudflats around the world (between 1924 and 1936, more than 175,000 plants from Arne Bay alone were sent to more than 130 sites). The grass has been in decline since the 1930s, and now more than half the original sward has gone. Once-muddy marshes near the Harbour mouth are now firm sands, a change which may be accelerated by rising sea levels.

Spartina grass, and its terrestrial equivalent, Japanese knotweed, are but two of the most conspicuous invaders of this delightful and essentially tranquil place. The invader with most potential for damage has had a remarkably small impact on this overcrowded corner of Dorset, and it is difficult to believe that the Harbour lies above the largest onshore oilfield in Europe. Those working the oilfield are committed to restoring the few sites they use, and will one day move on, leaving future observers as amazed as we are today when we are told that the pottery industry on the now peaceful island of Brownsea employed a workforce in the late 1800s of around 300 men.

A recent arrival in Dorset is the little egret, now a regular visitor to the mud-flats and marshes of Poole Harbour, and seen here in its breeding plumage.

BROWNSEA ISLAND

Of the five larger islands in the Harbour, Brownsea Island is the most remarkable. Its 200 hectares embrace a wide range of habitats, including acid grassland, heathland, pine woodland, two lakes, reedbed and alder carr, a brackish lagoon and a varied shoreline. The National Trust has owned the Island since 1962, leasing the northern half to the Dorset Wildlife Trust as a nature reserve and the castle to the John Lewis partnership.

The whole island is important for wildlife, probably the most famous being the remaining

Brownsea Island Quay, with part of the lagoon in the background.

population of red squirrels. Its island location and considerable Scots pine cover have protected this charming native animal from the invading grey squirrel, which has usurped it on its mainland sites. Red squirrels also survive on two of the other harbour islands – Green Island, and Furzey Island, where they were introduced some thirty years ago. Along with the Isle of Wight these remain the only sites for this endangered animal in southern England. Nightjar and woodcock nest in the heath and open woodland, whilst about 70 pairs of herons nest high up in the pines in the nature reserve.

The wetlands of Brownsea are of exceptional importance for wildlife. The lagoon has an important common and sandwich ternery and is host to thousands of waders during migration in winter. Nearly 700 avocets have over-wintered here, and other unusual waders such as ruff, curlew sandpiper, knot and black- and bar-tailed godwits are regular visitors. Hundreds of shelduck, wigeon and teal feed on the lagoon and the reedbeds support nesting reed warblers, reed

buntings, water rail and the declining water vole. Because of the variety of ponds and lakes on the Island, 17 species of dragonfly breed, including the spectacular downy emerald dragonfly, a local species seen in the spring. Rare fungi, insects, and lichens are still being discovered on this unusual island, where migrating ospreys often roost during the autumn. It is the only Dorset site for an endangered ant, *Myrmica schenki*, and the only place where a Mediterranean snail, *Papillaris papillifera*, lives in Britain.

The intriguing mix of terns, avocets, red squirrels, exotic trees and old buildings make the island a fascinating place to visit. Brownsea is easily accessible with boats running regularly in the spring and summer; paths are firm and dry and there are marked trails. The reserve has several bird hides, providing astounding views of nesting terns in midsummer. That Brownsea Island's unique quality has survived for our enjoyment today is a tribute to the National Trust and the Dorset Wildlife Trust, who both work hard to maintain its unique character.

Brownsea Island's most famous resident, a red squirrel.

TWO

MARINE WILDLIFE

MARINE HABITATS

As geologists and geomorphologists make the pilgrimage to the Dorset coast to study the rocks and coastal features, marine biologists, divers and those (like me!) who just like exploring rock pools visit in large numbers to study and enjoy the fascinating and colourful marine life. Even conservationists are sometimes guilty of referring to 'the marine habitat' alongside terrestrial habitats. You only need to dive off the Dorset coast or walk along the shore at low tide to realise that there are many different marine habitats supporting an amazing variety of wildlife. Many sea creatures appear strange and unfamiliar to us 'land-lubbers', but they are specially adapted to live in an environment which poses a whole different set of problems – waves, currents, salinity to name but a few.

So why can Dorset boast such abundant and interesting marine life? The varied geology and geomorphology of the coast has resulted in many different substrates – from soft muds and sands through shingle and cobble to hard rock ledges – which are colonised by marine wildlife. It also provides contrasting exposure to wave action, from the sheltered conditions of the upper reaches of Poole Harbour to the wave-battered shores of the Isle of Portland. The nearshore waters are relatively shallow, providing light conditions for

Waves breaking over the ledges in Kimmeridge Bay. The rocks and waters of the Bay form part of the Purbeck Marine Wildlife Reserve, Dorset's only underwater reserve.

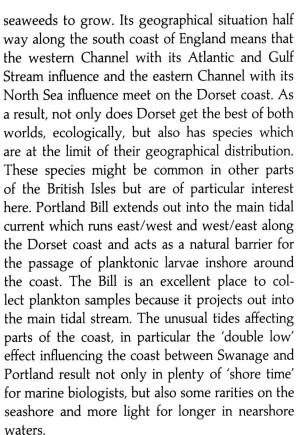

ABOVE *Lugworm casts on the Fleet at low tide.*

LEFT *Studland Bay at low tide.*

seaweeds to grow. Its geographical situation half way along the south coast of England means that the western Channel with its Atlantic and Gulf Stream influence and the eastern Channel with its North Sea influence meet on the Dorset coast. As a result, not only does Dorset get the best of both worlds, ecologically, but also has species which are at the limit of their geographical distribution. These species might be common in other parts of the British Isles but are of particular interest here. Portland Bill extends out into the main tidal current which runs east/west and west/east along the Dorset coast and acts as a natural barrier for the passage of planktonic larvae inshore around the coast. The Bill is an excellent place to collect plankton samples because it projects out into the main tidal stream. The unusual tides affecting parts of the coast, in particular the 'double low' effect influencing the coast between Swanage and Portland result not only in plenty of 'shore time' for marine biologists, but also some rarities on the seashore and more light for longer in nearshore waters.

BETWEEN THE TIDES

The seashore may seem a friendly place when we visit on summer holidays. It is, however, an extremely harsh environment in which to live. Intertidal marine life must contend with exposure to the drying effects of wind and sun and to predators such as birds and people when the tide is out, fluctuations in salinity of tide pools and the full force of the waves during a storm. Despite this many plants and animals are adapted to live here. So let us look at the diverse and varied habitats that occur between the tides.

SOFT SEDIMENT SHORES

Bearing in mind the problems intertidal plants and animals have to face, it is hardly surprising that most mobile animals on gravel, sand and muddy shores choose to live buried beneath the surface. You have to look carefully for clues to what lives there — a wormcast or empty shell. Animal life dominates sediment shores as there is no hard substrate for seaweeds to anchor themselves to.

SAND AND MUDDY SHORES

The shores of Poole Harbour have been described earlier in terms of their importance for birdlife and saltmarsh plant communities. We must not forget, however, that it is the marine life, buried in the sediments which provides food for wading birds. Polychaete worms such as the ragworm, and bivalve molluscs such as the edible cockle and sand gaper can be found beneath the surface of these shores. It is because so many animals make their home in the mud that it is so important to backfill the holes made during bait-digging. Look carefully at the strandlines in the upper reaches of Poole Harbour, too, and you will find they are littered with millions of tiny, whorled snail shells – the laver spire shell, *Hydrobia.* This minute snail lives on the surface of the mud and likes brackish water conditions.

SANDY BEACHES

The Dorset coast is spoilt for fine sandy beaches, as every tourist brochure tells us. However, Bournemouth's beaches are unstable, the sand being constantly washed away into Poole Bay and replenished. It is therefore a splendid place for sand castles but not for marine life. Studland and Shell Bay, however, are excellent places to exercise marine wildlife detective skills. Again you have to search for signs of what is buried beneath the surface – the safest place to live. Even at high tide, the strandline gives us plenty of clues. The molluscs we find on a sandy shore are bivalve, having two hinged shells, which can open to allow the animal to burrow and feed. Razor shells, carpet shells and the delicate thin tellin with colourful shells like butterfly wings can be commonly found, whilst the paper thin pandora shell is a speciality of Shell Bay.

On a very low spring tide, the siphons of razor shells can be seen on the surface of the sand at Studland and the shores of Portland Harbour, where sifting the sand reveals some tiny rarities. Lugworm casts can be seen low down on the shores of Studland, Weymouth, Portland Harbour, Charmouth and Lyme Regis. The worm lives in a U-shaped burrow below. The sand mason worm constructs a beautifully fashioned tube from sand and shell fragments. They look like tiny branched trees low down on the shore. If you are lucky, also at a very low tide, you might spot the masked crab, well camouflaged in the shallows and hermit crabs scuttling about in their borrowed shells.

The beach at Lyme Regis, looking east towards Golden Cap.

LEFT *The fruiting bladder wrack.*

BELOW *Japweed, an alien arrival in the 1970s, crowding out native seaweeds in Kimmeridge Bay.*

BOULDER AND ROCKY SHORES

There are excellent examples of these shorelines in Dorset. They are the perfect locations for marine life enthusiasts. Many different habitats can be found here and the plants and animals are specially adapted to fill their particular niche on the shore. At a glance, the most obvious difference between rocky and sandy shores is the domination by seaweeds. The strandline at high water mark, after a storm, may have drift weed piled high – not very pleasant for us but delicious for the seaweed flies and shore-hoppers who live in it.

The familiar brown seaweeds on the rocks and boulders of the shore are the wracks. These and certain animals associated with them are recognised as being indicators of the exposure of the shore to wave action and they grow in zones down the beach. The wracks in Dorset have not read the text books, and the zones overlap! This is actually due to the small tidal range and horizontal nature of our shores. On the upper shore, the spiralled wrack dries up when the tide is out but 'reconstitutes' when submerged again. The bladder wrack with its gas-filled bladders to buoy it in the water dominates the mid-shore, and the serrated wrack with its saw edges can be found on the lower shore. The rubbery egg wrack dominates on Dorset's more sheltered shores.

Rocky shores of Dorset exhibit a good variety of colourful seaweeds, including several species at the edge of their geographical distribution. The filamentous, green sea lettuce contrasts with the coarse pink coralline weed in rock pools. Sea lettuce and other green algae growing abnormally abundantly is a good indication of excess nutrients, in particular nitrates from farmland, entering the water. This is particularly evident in the Fleet. Lower shore rock pools are encrusted with the rock-hard, pink, calcareous *Lithothamnion sp.* and the dark green, tufted *Cladophora rupestris.* Specialities of the Dorset coast are the stunning, iridescent weed *Cystoseira tamariscifolia*, glowing blue or purple in the sunlight, the spongy, green fingers of *Codium fragile* and the annual peacock's tail weed.

A recent arrival on the Dorset coast is 'japweed', an alien seaweed brought to this country in the 1970s on the hull of a ship or with imported oysters. It now thrives in rock pools and in shallow water the length of Dorset. It requires a hard substrate but settles for empty shells or even ring-pulls in the Fleet. Rafts or strings of the drift weed can be seen floating on the surface. In addition to being an amenity problem in harbours and the Fleet, becoming tangled in boat propellers and fishing nets, 'japweed' is having an ecological impact, crowding out native weeds.

Animals commonly seen on Dorset's rocky shores are snails such as rough periwinkles, the tiny small periwinkles on the more exposed ledges of the upper shore and the brightly coloured flat periwinkles, well camouflaged on the wracks. Shells can be deceptive, and if you are collecting them make sure they are empty!

Limpets graze the surface of ledges and boulders with their nail-file tongues. At Kimmeridge you can clearly see the zig-zag grazing marks on the limestone. A conservation project here, run by the Dorset Wildlife Trust, includes a 'Limpet Protection Zone'. On exposed headlands limpets have more flattened shells than those of their counterparts in sheltered bays – an evolutionary trend resulting in a better shape to survive powerful wave action.

In rock pools, the striped purple topshell and common winkle are common. The dog whelk preys on winkles, and other shells and barnacles, by drilling a hole through the shell and sucking out the unfortunate victim. Dog whelk eggs, resembling tiny milk bottles can be seen commonly under overhangs. Barnacles cover the rocks on more exposed shores and on groynes and sea walls. The acorn barnacle dominates but other species found include the alien Australian barnacle *Elminius modestus*.

Shore crabs can be found lurking under rocks and seaweed at all levels. On the lower shore, the fierce velvet swimming crab, with its flattened swimming legs and bright red eyes can be found under overhangs and is particularly common at Charmouth and Lyme Regis. Prawns are a common sight once your eyes become trained to see these transparent creatures. A visit to the shore on a very low tide is rewarded with broad-clawed porcelain 'crabs', clinging to the undersides of boulders, and squat lobsters which scuttle away with a flip of the tail. Hermit crabs are a common sight in the rock pools.

Common anemones are the beadlet anemone – the green, red and, less commonly, strawberry forms. These are found from the mid-shore down to extreme low water mark and a few large specimens can be found below the tide level at Swanage Pier. Snakelocks anemones, with their long snake-like tentacles, dominate in rock pools and in shallow water. A word of warning – touching the tentacles of this creature can result in an allergic reaction, especially in children. The dahlia anemone, its body 'decorated' with fragments of shell and stone, can be found in low shore pools in west Dorset.

Starfish to be found in rock pools are the tiny, delicate brittle star (but you need sharp eyes to see them) and the small cushion star, a less common sight. The green sea urchin is at the edge of its distribution in west Dorset. Broad Ledge at Lyme Regis is a good place to find these under low shore boulders.

Other unlikely-looking animals to be found on the seashore include breadcrumb and purse sponges and the electric light bulb sea squirt. Finally, we must not forget the fish. Rock gobies and blennies dwell in rock pools. Blennies can sit out of water at low tide, and the ugly short-spined sea scorpion is a dramatic find. The Cornish sucker clings to the rocks in low shore pools in the western part of the county.

The snakelocks anemone is common in rock pools and shallow water.

LEFT *The distinctive blue-rayed limpet, seen here in a group lit by early morning light at low tide.*

ABOVE *A ballan wrasse tucked up asleep underneath a rock in Kimmeridge Bay.*

BENEATH THE WAVES

THE SHALLOWS

On our rocky coastline, the shallow water is dominated by kelp. Described as 'the kelp forest', these huge seaweeds are the watery equivalent of trees on land. Many other seaweeds (epiphytes), such as the delicate red weed *Polysiphonia violacea*, grow on the stipe (stalk) of the kelp and animals can be found on the fronds (leaves) and in the holdfasts. The blue-rayed limpet, with its vivid blue stripes, is a common find – the young ones on the fronds and the adults in the holdfasts. It is always worth looking for these in fresh holdfasts, washed up after a storm. Bristly, fabric-like seamat often covers the fronds, and holdfasts often harbour small crabs, sponges and the jelly-like star sea squirt.

In these shallow, rocky areas, dominated by kelp and a smaller brown weed, sea oak, which thrives in the Kimmeridge area, where the shale bedrock can be too unstable for the heavy kelp, colourful corkwing and ballan wrasse weave their way amongst the weeds. The male lump sucker, a large, bony fish, guards his eggs in shallow water. The spiny spider crab arrives in the shallows in the spring and in the summer congregates in huge mounds to moult and mate. These mounds are a particular feature of the west Dorset coast and the moulted shells, washed up on the shore in large numbers, are often mistaken for a mass mortality.

DEEPER LEDGES

On the offshore bedrock and boulders at greater depths there is no longer enough light for the larger seaweeds to grow. This habitat is dominated by the smaller red seaweeds such as *Phyllophora crispa*. Deeper again, there is even less light and the boulders and ledges are covered with sponges such as the orange latticework sponge, sea squirts and hornwrack, a biscuit-coloured leafy form, looking for all the world like a seaweed, and the closely related ross coral. These bryozoans are actually colonies of tiny box-like animals. Attractive anemones like the daisy-like *Actinotho sphyrodeta* and *Sagartia elegans* contrast with equally colourful sponges. Fish to be seen here include the leopard-spotted goby and tompot blenny in rock crevices and the cuckoo wrasse; the male in his breeding colours is a spectacular sight.

Rocky ledges are a feature of much of the Dorset coast and these continue out under the sea. The softer rock ledges are often riddled with holes, bored by a bivalve mollusc with a delightful name, the boring piddock. You can see these for yourself, without having to go diving, on the ledges at Charmouth at low tide. Have you ever picked up a 'lucky stone' with a hole through it on the beach? Now you know who bored it! In addition to providing horizontal surfaces for weeds and plant-like animals to colonise, the ledges also provide vertical surfaces – a very different habitat. These are covered with animals such as the fanworm *Bispira volutacornis*, sea squirts and encrusting sponges. Under overhangs, edible crabs, lobsters and conger eels hide.

AN UNDERWATER DESERT?

Shell gravel and sand is often perceived as an underwater desert by divers. On close inspection, however, they are interesting habitats in their own right. The scavenger, the common whelk, can be found here and its empty shells are quickly occupied by hermit crabs, many with anemones on their shells. A smaller whelk, the netted dog whelk, is especially common in Dorset. Edible scallops lie just beneath the surface of the sand, many of which are collected by divers or dredged in Lyme Bay. This latter method of fishing has had a serious impact, not only on the scallop population, but also on other seabed communities. The smaller queen and variegated scallops also occur off the Dorset coast, 'dancing' above the seabed.

West Dorset fishermen can pin-point, precisely, areas of seabed where the strange bulky scale worm, the sea mouse, are brought up in large numbers in their nets. These beautiful, iridescent animals are superstitiously treated with respect.

SPECIAL MARINE HABITATS

Off the Purbeck coast are areas of seabed dominated by the calcareous alga, *Phymatolithon calcarium*, or maerl. This is a specialised habitat because the knobbly skeletons of the dead alga build up on the seabed and create an environment for other species to live. Dorset also boasts extensive beds of eel grass species. Particularly famous is that in the Fleet, whilst there are also beds off Studland. This is the only flowering plant that lives in the sea and associated with it are pipe fish and various molluscs.

MAN-MADE HABITATS

Marine life is quick to colonise any suitable man-made structure, as any boat-owner will know! The piles of Swanage Pier are an underwater photographer's paradise. Shaded by the pier itself, they are colonised by the invertebrates you would normally have to dive to some depth to see. They are covered with sponges, plumose anemones, dead man's fingers, fan-worms and much, much more. Dorset's wrecks are similarly covered and also attract shoals of pout. The breakwater around Portland Harbour provides a habitat for several rarities, including the shy black-faced blenny. In Poole Bay, an experimental artificial reef has been laid on the seabed by Southampton University to study colonisation by marine life.

As you can see, there is a wealth of fascinating marine wildlife under Dorset's seas, but we cannot return to dry land without mentioning Dorset's larger marine visitors. Durlston Coastwatch at Durlston Country Park, Swanage, keeps a visual and acoustic record of whales and dolphins passing along the Purbeck coast. Bottle-nosed dolphins are frequent visitors, spotted by volunteer watchers as frequently as one day in three, and common dolphins and pilot whales are also being heard on the hydrophone.

Bispira volutacornis, *a variety of fan worm.*

THREE
THE HEATHS

THE HISTORICAL HEATH

Would it have ever been possible to persuade John Claridge to see heathland with different eyes? It was he, an itinerant traveller of the eighteenth century who, visiting Dorset in 1793, described our heaths as 'a most dreary waste'. In truth he was experiencing something that many of us would regard as a privilege, namely that of seeing the Dorset heaths in their undiminished glory. His eyes were able to see unbroken purple and golden heathland stretching from his feet to the horizon. His eyes, had he but wished to look, could have seen a wealth of wildlife which we can now only dream about.

Claridge and others bemoaned what they saw as the wild and quite untamed nature of the heath, failing to appreciate that not only was man then having a considerable influence upon it, but that he had been largely responsible for creating it in the first place! Examination of

Tadnoll Nature Reserve, adjoining Winfrith Heath and owned by the Dorset Wildlife Trust. The heaths of Dorset are examples of 'European lowland heathland'. Such heathland is naturally restricted to the eastern coast of Europe from southern Sweden to northern Spain including the British Isles. Here it is confined to areas of central, southern and eastern England, including the London and Hampshire Basins. Where the Hampshire Basin crosses into eastern Dorset it is known as the Poole Basin. The Tertiary Bagshot and Bracklesham Beds of the Poole Basin comprise a variety of highly inhospitable sands and gravels interspersed with clay, and it is upon these that the heaths of Dorset were formed. The Dorset heaths are exceptionally rich in habitats and species, and are thus highly prized as outstanding examples of a nationally and internationally rare habitat.

pollen preserved in the peat bogs of south-east Dorset shows that in the distant past the vegetation was, just like most of the rest of the British Isles, dominated by woodland – albeit probably a rather lighter cover of woodland than elsewhere, reflecting the naturally inhospitable parent soils on which it was growing.

Mesolithic man, even with his simple hunting and gathering activities, seemingly further opened up this light woodland cover, while Bronze Age man had little difficulty in clearing it altogether – and in so doing created the heaths.

This Bronze Age heath formation is evidenced by the sudden increase in heather and grass pollen at the expense of tree pollen preserved in the peat of the local bogs, and by the abundance of heather and grass pollen in the Bronze Age soils preserved beneath round barrows – many of which are to be found on the heaths. Once the trees had been lost and the heath had taken over, the naturally acid and nutrient poor soils could only become more acid and impoverished, preventing the return of woodland and maintaining the dominance of heath. In any case man's activities maintained the change. From then on he used and abused the heath he had created for his own ends and, as we shall see, the wildlife of the heath developed with and blossomed under his rule.

Man put the heaths to a variety of uses. They provided rough low intensity grazing for livestock, including horses (Hardy's heath-croppers), cattle and possibly some sheep. Deliberate small scale burning, to encourage the growth of palatable young heather and grasses, may have been associated with the grazing, at least to some degree. Bracken was gathered to provide bedding for the livestock.

Dorset is without coal and the region was by then largely devoid of true woodland, so the heath had to provide its inhabitants with fuel – which it did in the form of both turf and peat. 'Turbary' rights carefully defined how much of these fuels could be taken and were fiercely defended. Gorse was also cut, the older stems for

fuel and the young shoots for fodder. From under the heath the local people took small quantities of sand and gravel for their needs.

Clay, which occurs in localised lenses beneath the heath, was also dug on a small scale. Attempts were of course often made to change the heath into true agricultural land, but the soils were such that the enterprise was normally short-lived, and before too long the land would again become 'covered with furze and ling'. In the absence of fencing wood or stone, marking boundaries on the heath in relation to these many uses was achieved by the digging of banks and ditches – many of which can still be seen criss-crossing the heathland.

All these activities combined to affect the heath in a number of ways. Most importantly the turf cutting and grazing, possibly associated with burning, had the vital effect of constantly depleting nutrients so that more demanding non-heathland plants would be prevented from replacing the tolerant heathland ones. Any scrubby vegetation which did establish would, in any case, be removed by these activities. Thus by these means the heath was maintained in its open, largely treeless state. Secondly these three key activities were constantly 'resetting' parts of the heathland vegetation.

Heathland left to its own devices will progress through various phases of growth which ecologists have labelled as pioneer, building, and mature. At any time during this progression, intervention can set it back to the pioneer stage. The three activities would have ensured that the heath had representation of all the growth stages – what is now called a 'diverse age structure'. This is significant, since, as we shall see, many elements of the heathland flora and fauna are associated with different stages of the heath. A diverse age structure thus maximises species diversity. Thirdly, and perhaps most interestingly, all the various activities created a whole range of specialised niches which the individual species, both plant and animal, could exploit.

PLANT COMMUNITIES

As his carriage rolled onwards in quest of more promising terrain, John Claridge apparently only spared a passing glance for the nature of the heath he was crossing. He and other travellers saw only what to them was a monotonous expanse of 'furze, fern and ling'. If only they had looked a little closer! They could have seen a remarkable range of different habitats, changing continuously from one to another depending on the wetness of the terrain and on the uses to which the heath was then being put.

DRY HEATH

The higher freely draining sands and gravels support dry heath, the flora of which is delightfully simple. It is normally dominated by the common heather or ling *(Calluna vulgaris)* with its tiny very pale flowers, with a proportion of the more strongly coloured bell heather *(Erica cinerea)*. The only other faithful component is a dwarf gorse – and which of the two British species present will depend on exactly where you are. The heaths from Christchurch to Cranborne and from Wareham to Dorchester have the gentle eastern dwarf gorse *(Ulex minor)*, whereas the block of heaths in the middle, around Poole and Bournemouth, have the ferocious western dwarf gorse *(Ulex gallii)*. As the names indicate these species have segregated distributions in the British Isles, and Dorset is unusual in having both because their ranges overlap in the mid-south, but this fascinating separation of the two within Dorset has yet to be explained! Sometimes the heather or gorse will look as though red cotton has been strewn over it. This is the remarkable dodder *(Cuscuta epithymum)*, a parasitic plant which takes its nutrients from its host and, needing no chlorophyll, has red stems supporting its

The tiny pinkish white flowers of the dodder, a parasitic plant that attaches itself with suckers to the stem of its host, usually gorse or heather, and flowers between July and October.

clustered pinkish white flowers. The grass of the dry heath is the small and very fine leaved bristle bent *(Agrostis curtisii)* and this may become dominant after a fire. Further botanising on the dry heath will provide only a scattering of additional higher plant records. The tiny blue flower of the heath milkwort *(Polygala serpyllifolia)* is well worth searching for and a really careful examination of the sandy exposures of old trackways and mineral workings could reveal the scarce mossy stonecrop *(Crassula tillaea)*, the first of the many heathland species to be taking advantage of the special niches created by man. Outside Dorset this little plant occurs only in other heathlands in the New Forest and East Anglia.

It would be quite unfair to leave the dry heath, however, without a mention of the mosses and lichens. The dry heath supports a number of these lower plants and indeed the lichen flora is quite special. These include a number of *Cladonia* species, such as *Cladonia floerkeana* ('devil's matches') with its bright red fruiting bodies, which are particularly in evidence. Bracken *(Pteridium aquilinum)* is of course widespread. Its occurrence is thought to be related to at least a small degree of soil enrichment.

HUMID AND WET HEATH

A keen botanist released on the Dorset heathlands is not then likely to spend too long on the dry heath, but will gravitate quickly to the lower ground where the water table is naturally high or where a lens of clay within the sands and gravels impedes drainage. For the scientist the crucial indicator of the change to wet heath will be the appearance of two of the less conspicuous bog mosses *(Sphagnum compactum* and

S. *tenellum)*, but the more visual change arises from the replacement of the ling and bell heather with the grey-green foliage of the cross-leaved heath *(Erica tetralix)*. At the same time the bristle bent grass is replaced with the larger and wider stemmed purple moor grass *(Molinia caerulea)*. As with the dry heath it is the grassy element which dominates after a fire.

Relatively common on the wet heaths, but special because of its bright yellow splendour, is the bog asphodel *(Narthecium ossifragum)*. Even later in the year the strong orange of its fruiting head adds colour to the wetland. Here the sedges and rushes really come into their own, with deer sedge *(Trichophorum cespitosum)*, white beaked sedge *(Rhynchospora alba)* and the many stalked spike rush *(Eleocharis multicaulis)* being certain finds on most sites. The wet heath is also the main home of the insectivorous sundews *(Drosera spp.)*. Dorset can boast all three British sundews since the rarest, the great sundew *(D. anglica)*, occurs on

OPPOSITE TOP *The cross-leaved heath. The change from ling and bell heather to cross-leaved heath is a good indicator of the transition from dry to wet heath.*

LEFT *Bog asphodel at Coombe Heath.*

RIGHT *Dorset's heaths are home to all three British sundews, of which the great sundew is the rarest. Insects are trapped by the sticky gland-tipped hairs on the leaves and then digested.*

Dorset heath. (Erica ciliaris) The low-growing Dorset heath is rarely found outside the Purbeck heathlands.

The marsh gentian, one of Dorset's rarer flowers, which grows in open well-grazed damp heath.

a number of the Dorset heaths. The sundews are separated by the shape of the leaf, but all have the fine hairs which secrete a sticky substance upon which surprisingly large unsuspecting insects become trapped and drained of their nutrients. An enterprising way to supplement the diet on these nutrient poor systems!

The wet heath is not only where the botanist will find more plants, but also more of the rare and scarce ones. While the white beaked sedge may be relatively widespread nationally and in Dorset, the brown beaked sedge *(Rhynchospora fusca)* is a much rarer species both inside and outside the county. On the heathlands in and around Purbeck, but rarely beyond, the cross-leaved heath may be joined by its much rarer cousin, our very own Dorset heath *(Erica ciliaris)*. This striking, deep coloured heather has a UK distribution which is almost entirely limited to Dorset and the reason for its curious national and Dorset distribution is yet another interesting source of debate.

A close contender for pride of place in the Dorset heathland flora is the marsh gentian *(Gentiana pneumonanthe)*. Its beautiful blue trumpet shaped flowers grace a scattering of our wet heaths in the late summer and early autumn. Although the plant occurs relatively widely on other heaths in the British Isles, the Dorset heaths are the stronghold of this remarkable plant. While it is not certain why marsh gentian occurs on some wet heaths and not others, it is evident that it is one of the several species which likes an open vegetation structure and that its numbers diminish with time after fire and cessation of grazing. Similarly, but even more so, the rare marsh clubmoss *(Lycopodiella inundata)* only occurs when poaching or other disturbance provides bare peat for it to establish. It too is very much dependent upon the Dorset heaths for its national survival and even here less than 15 sites are now known. The heath lobelia *(Lobelia urens)* shows similar ephemeral tendencies within its restricted national distribution and within its now single Dorset location. Add to this the fact that two of the sundews are most prolific on exposed peat, and it is immediately

evident that the more special wet heathland plants are very much dependent upon bare ground, or at least an open vegetation structure, which in turn is dependent upon man's traditional uses of the heath.

There is an intermediate heathland habitat which is still dry enough to be dominated by ling, but just wet enough to support a good scattering of cross-leaved heath. It is aptly called humid or damp heathland and can cover quite extensive areas where the ground conditions are thus finely balanced.

BOGS, POOLS AND STREAMS

Peat bog, or acid mire, develops in the very wettest of areas where decomposition is so reduced that peat accumulates — often to a considerable depth. Most of the plants of the wet heath also grow here, but the extreme wetness brings in a number of additional and intriguing species.

The essential ingredients are the larger bog mosses (*Sphagnum spp.*). The specialised hyaline cells hold water like a sponge and no educational visit to the heath can be complete without

Open water and bog, the Hartland Moor National Nature Reserve near Corfe Castle.

The bog pimpernel is a small creeping perennial. It is still relatively common in Dorset, and its delicate pink flowers are one of the delights of the wetter parts of the heath.

Bog orchids in flower on Hartland Moor. The bog orchid is only a few inches high, and has a spike of tiny yellowish-green flowers which are twisted so that the lip points upwards.

vulgaris) has not been seen for many a year. But the very special rarity for bog has to be the bog orchid *(Hammarbya paludosa)*. A mainly northern species, this tiny orchid is known from just a handful of sites in Dorset where it finds a home on the open *Sphagnum* carpets. Rarer still, the bog hair grass *(Deschampsia setacea)* is now known from only two locations in Dorset where conditions are both wet and open.

Small streams and ditches frequently drain through and from the bogs while their surfaces and surrounds are often scattered with pools and ponds – most of which have their origin in man's former activities of peat, sand, gravel and clay digging. These flowing and still waters provide two further special habitats. Here can be found yet another plant with a carnivorous diet – the aptly named bladderwort *(Utricularia spp.)* whose tiny lidded bladders suck in insects suspended in the water. Like the sundews, Dorset can boast all the British species.

SCRUB

Before moving to the fauna of the heath, special mention must be made of the scrub habitats, not least because they are a key element in supporting the heathland fauna, particularly invertebrates and birds. Common gorse *(Ulex europaeus)* distinguishes itself from the dwarf gorses by growing as a large winter-flowering shrub whose distribution is closely associated with man's past activities. Old mineral workings and boundary banks are often demarcated by gorse scrub. Left to its own devices gorse eventually becomes open and leggy, but fortunately it responds well to rejuvenation by cutting or burning. While gorse is the classic shrub of dry heath, that of the wet heath and bog is the sweet gale *(Myrica gale)*, so called because of the delightful fragrance it emits when crushed.

Pine, birch, willow and broom are further important components of the heathland scrub. However, in recent times at least, all have shown a tendency to exceed their welcome by invading the open heath.

a demonstration of how much water can be squeezed out of a handful of bog moss!

The white tufts bobbing over the bog will usually be those of the common cotton grass *(Eriophorum angustifolium)*, but occasionally they will be those of the harestail *(E. vaginatum)* which, though generally a northern species, does extend its range into parts of Dorset. The bog is also the place to search for a second insectivorous plant, the pale butterwort *(Pinguicula lusitanica)* which also uses sticky leaves to trap insects. While the slender white flower of the sundew is unfortunately often overlooked, the pale violet-like flower of the butterwort is one of the most memorable sights on the heath. Sadly the stronger coloured flower of the common butterwort *(P.*

ANIMALS OF THE HEATH

While a botanist may gravitate to the wet heath and bog, a zoologist will find more than enough of interest on the dry heath to keep him content – although he will undoubtedly want to spend a good deal of time in the wetlands as well!

ANTS, WASPS AND BEETLES

Certainly the heathland invertebrates have fully exploited the whole range of habitats and specialised their niches. By rights, of course, the invertebrates should occupy a starring role throughout this book, and particularly here, since the Dorset heathlands are outstandingly rich in this enormous assortment of creatures. But space forces us to ignore many groups in favour of the few.

Ants have the privilege of being particularly well studied on the Dorset heaths and the interrelationships of the five black heathland ants, *Tetramorium caespitum, Lasius alienus, L. niger, Formica fusca* and *F. transkaucaisica* and the three red ones, *Myrmica ruginodis, M. scabrinodis* and *M. sabuleti*, have made a fascinating study. These species not only divide the heath in relation to the dryness or wetness of conditions, but in relation to the stage of the heath. For example *L. niger* uses the wet heath while *L. alienus* and *T. caespitum* both occupy the dry. However *L. alienus* is most abundant in the pioneer dry heath and declines thereafter, whereas *T. caespitum* does best in the more mature dry heath. Give an ant specialist a sample of ants from an area of heath and he should be able to predict its type and age from the analysis of species present! The ants of the Dorset heaths include rare and scarce species. In particular, the bog ant *(Formica candida)* is found only on sphagnum bogs in Dorset and the New Forest while two species which are parasitic upon *T. caespitum* are also rare. Some other species have probably already become extinct.

The strongly coloured velvet ant *(Mutilla europaea)* which may be regularly seen on the Dorset heaths, is not in truth an ant at all, but one of the many wasps which live there. The velvet ant lays its eggs on bee grubs in the bees' own nests and the wasp larvae will feed upon them on hatching. However, the true Digger wasps actually capture and store various prey for their larvae, often in the security of their specially prepared burrows. The spider-hunting wasps, as the name suggests, specialise in the storage of spiders. The mining bees are also well represented on the heathland. The availability of warm open sand, usually as a result of the many forms of ground disturbances created by man's former use of it, is then a vital factor in rendering the Dorset heathlands so rich in these fascinating excavating invertebrates. Heather and bumble bees are almost synonymous, and indeed the heaths are rich in these species which, in some cases, have to bite their way into the bases of flowers, leaving a tell-tale hole behind.

Beetles, including the tiger beetles and the weevils, are numerous on the heathlands. The green tiger beetle (*Cicindela campestris*) and wood tiger beetle (*C. sylvatica*), like the excavating bees and wasps, need those dry sandy exposures for burrow making. By contrast the much rarer and most beautiful beetle, *Carabus nitens*, which occurs primarily on the heaths of Dorset and the

The green tiger beetle lives in burrows on dry sandy heath.

New Forest, has a preference for the wet heaths. Weevils occur in all the habitats and many are particularly associated with scrub. Scrub is actually rich in many invertebrates, making it a valued component of the heath in its own right and a key element in the food chain.

SPIDERS

There are more species of spider on Dorset heathland than on any other habitat in Britain, exploiting every possible niche from the dry sandy heath to the water of the bog pools. Several are true heathland specialists and exceedingly rare. For *Altella lucida* and *Eresus niger* the single dry heathland locations in Dorset are also the only sites for the species in the country. *Alopecosa fabrilis* has the security of one other site in Surrey, while *Cheiracanthium pennyi* is rather more abundant there, but otherwise has only one other site – in Dorset. *Ero aphana* and *Haplodrassus umbratilis* both have their strongholds in the New Forest and the less than half a dozen heathland sites in east Dorset. In contrast to these mainly dry heathland species *Zora armillata* occurs on two bogs in Dorset – and a few fens in East Anglia. Of these great rarities only *Eresus niger* is obliging enough to have a common name – the ladybird spider – reflecting the huge spotted abdomen of the female, who never emerges from her burrow.

Species which a casual visitor to the heath might reasonably hope to encounter and readily recognize include *Araneus quadratus* displaying its four spotted abdomen in assorted colourways, *Agroeca proxima* leaving its distinctive white egg sacks hanging from the heather, *Atypus affinis* lurking in the vortex of its funnelled web, *Dolomedes fimbriatus* poised at the edge of bog pools waiting for potential prey, and *Argiope bruennichi* with its huge and dramatically striped yellow and black abdomen. The last species, a wolf spider, has recently joined us from Europe and has made itself very much at home on the Dorset heaths.

GRASSHOPPERS AND CRICKETS

On a summer's day the heath veritably buzzes with the sound of grasshoppers and crickets. Many will also be found in other Dorset habitats, but they include three which can claim to be heathland faithfuls, and, of these, two are national rarities while the third is at least scarce.

The heath grasshopper (Chorthippus vagans) is virtually restricted to the heaths of Dorset and the New Forest. Its habitat requirements are not well understood, but certainly it is a creature of the dry heath and seems to be associated with habitat transitions within it. At the opposite extreme of the habitat range, the large marsh grasshopper (Stethophyma grossum) definitely likes the very wettest areas — seemingly associated with carpets of sphagnum in the valley bogs. Its distribution is only a little wider than that of the heath grasshopper.

Our most special cricket must be the bog bush cricket (Metrioptera brachyptera). Although very much a heathland species it is happily unparticular within it, occurring widely over both dry and wet heathland habitats.

DRAGONFLIES AND DAMSELFLIES

For both dragonflies and damselflies the Dorset heathlands are undoubtedly one of the richest habitats in the country. This is a reflection of Dorset's southern location and warm climate, the tolerance shown by many British species to acidic conditions, and the number and variety of essential breeding sites on and around the heathlands. The tiny sphagnum flushes of the bogs are enough for some. Others use the flowing waters of the streams and ditches. Many have readily taken advantage of the still waters of the numerous pools, ponds and lakes created by man's activities — peat cutting, small-scale mineral winning etc. Thus, here again, the use and abuse by man has contributed to the special wealth of wildlife that we are so fortunate to find today.

There are some half a dozen species which are particularly strongly tied to the heathland. The small red damselfly (Ceriagrion tenellum) is perhaps most strongly linked. It utilises the small sphagnum flushes, and is also the most rare on a national basis, being confined to the heathlands of Dorset, Hampshire, Surrey and Sussex. By contrast

A bog bush cricket. It is active on Dorset's heath from July to October, and its 'song' is a repetitive shrill chirp, five or six per second, which can last for minutes on end.

A small red damselfly, which lives on the sphagnum mosses on the heath and is now only found in a handful of southern counties.

The keeled skimmer dragonfly resting on bog asphodel.

the black darter *(Sympetrum danae)* is nationally widespread, being associated with both upland moorland and lowland heathland. It is the most common species to be seen on the heathlands in the autumn – but rarely beyond them. Similarly the common hawker *(Aeshna juncea)* and keeled skimmer *(Orthetrum coerulescens)* are relatively widespread nationally but closely linked with the heaths in Dorset. The heathlands are also the place to see the downy emerald *(Cordulia aenea)*, but the ponds which they utilise must be sheltered by trees or scrub. Finally special mention should be made of the southern damselfly *(Coenagrion mercuriale)* and scarce blue-tailed damselfly *(Ischnura pumilio)*, both national rarities whose specialised transitory habitat requirements are sometimes met on the Dorset heathlands.

BUTTERFLIES AND MOTHS

The one group the heathlands cannot claim to be rich in is the butterflies! No matter, because the butterfly most commonly associated with heathland is particularly well-represented in Dorset. The beautiful silver-studded blue *(Plebejus argus)*, like its more famous cousin, the large blue

(Maculinea arion), has a complex and fascinating life style. The butterfly larvae initially feed upon young heathers and gorses but are later actually taken into the nests of one of the black heathland ants, either *Lasius alienus* or *L. niger*. The pupae are buried in ant cells and the ants have been observed attending the adults until they take flight – over relatively short distances only. Not surprisingly the colonies of the silver-studded blue are very localised and their strong association with immature dry to wet heathland reflects the related requirements of both butterfly and ant. This butterfly is able to exploit similar conditions on a few calcareous grasslands in Dorset and is a special feature of the limestone grasslands of Portland.

While the silver-studded blue may be our very special heathland species, two other butterflies cannot be ignored. Walking along a dry heathland path in summer will almost certainly be rewarded by an easy introduction to the grayling *(Hipparchia semele)*. This large butterfly will sit on the open ground where its grey mottling and careful angling to the sun will render it virtually invisible. As you approach it will unexpectedly rise up, only to settle again a few paces further on. No other butterfly will offer so many easy chances for

The beautiful silver-studded blue butterfly.

The large emerald moth is found in woods and on heathland where birches are plentiful.

pug (*Erpithecia goossensiata*), narrow-winged pug (*E. nanata*), yellow underwing (*Anarta myrtilli*) and the true-lovers knot (*Lychophotia porphyrea*) amongst many others. One night's light trapping at Higher Hyde Heath in July produced no less than 194 different species! The speckled footman (*Coscinia cribraria*) was first discovered in Dorset and subsequent records have revealed it to be very much confined to our heathlands and those of the New Forest. Of the many micro moths found on heathland a small space must be reserved for the remarkable bag worm (*Pachythelia villosella*), whose females never leave the caddis fly-like cases which they construct from heather litter.

REPTILES AND AMPHIBIANS

a good view! In late spring the heathland also offers the ready prospect of seeing our only green butterfly the green hairstreak (*Callophrys rubi*), as its larvae feed on gorse and broom.

The relative paucity of heathland butterflies is compensated for by the moths. Daytime observation will be rewarded by sightings of the common heath (*Ematurga atomaria*), the foxmoth (*Macrothylacia rubi*) and the males of the emperor moth (*Saturnia pavonia*), but the effort of light-trapping will reveal the abundance of the night flying ling

Those in search of the most famous occupant of Dorset heathland – surely the sand lizard (*Lacerta agilis*) – will head for dry heath, especially dry heath where old mineral workings, boundary banks, or other disturbances have left an uneven terrain with open sand. After emergence in spring the male turns bright green to attract the female, who then lays and buries her eggs in exposed sand. South facing slopes where the warmth will assist incubation are favoured, and it matters little whether the southerly aspect results from natural

The rarest and most famous of all the residents of Dorset's heaths is the sand lizard, seen here basking on a log.

slopes or small scale disturbances by man. Because such habitats tend to be localised, and because sand lizards are strongly territorial in their attachment to their burrows and modest feeding ground, they are often described as occurring in 'colonies'. The young lizards hatch around May and disperse into the surrounding heather to feed up on assorted invertebrates before they go, a little after the adults, into winter hibernation. They are easily distinguished from common lizards (*Lacerta vivipara*) by their larger size, stouter outline and bold back markings — individuals can even be identified from their unique patterning.

Smooth snakes (*Coronella austriaca*) have much larger territories than sand lizards, and do not have the open sand requirement, giving birth to live young. Sand lizards have the helpful habit of basking at the sides of tracks or clearings where they may be relatively easy to see — especially the males in spring. Few of us however will see the secretive smooth snake in the wild and must be consoled by the fact that they are relatively unremarkable — a brown/grey body with darker splodges down the sides, quite different from the boldly marked adder (*Vipera berus*) or the yellow-collared grass snake (*Natrix natrix*). Since each of these reptiles, and the slow worm (*Anguis fragilis*), occur on the heathlands of Dorset, the habitat has the special attribute of supporting all our native reptiles.

It probably appears to the road or house builder that sand lizards and smooth snakes occupy every acre of Dorset heathland. Though both are exceedingly rare outside the county, they are still luckily surviving, against considerable odds, on most of the Dorset heaths where their special requirements are met. It is estimated that Dorset supports 80% of the national population of sand lizards, with only modest populations occurring on some heathlands to the east and a single separate population just surviving on the sand dunes of Lancashire. Similarly the Dorset smooth snake population represents about 90% of the UK total. There is just a touch of irony in knowing

The adder is Britain's only poisonous snake, and is easily identified by the zigzag pattern on its back.

that the diet of the smooth snake includes the sand lizard!

The Dorset heaths are actually not a particularly good habitat for amphibians. Although the waters they require for breeding are abundant, by virtue of the assortment of former land-uses, the majority are quite strongly acidic. Only the palmate newt (*Triturus helveticus*) seemingly favours acid waters, and is consequently the most commonly occurring amphibian of the heathlands.

The very rare natterjack toad (*Bufo calamita*) did once breed naturally in Dorset, although probably never extensively. Like the sand lizard it favours both heathland and coastal dunes, and does still survive in these habitats in several other counties. Although lost from Dorset for a time the toad has now been successfully re-introduced to two sites: one of which is one of the few Dorset sites in which it was definitely recorded in the past.

A Dartford warbler. Hard winters in the early 1960s cut the entire British population to ten pairs, virtually all of them in Dorset. The numbers are now on the increase, but it remains one of our rarest breeding birds, building its nest in gorse or tall heather.

BIRDS

The special birds of the Dorset heathland are special indeed, not just because they are so rare, but because they are individualists with highly distinctive characters and life styles. A frustrated road supporter was once heard to protest that Dartford warblers turned up at every public inquiry he had ever been to! The image evoked of this pert little bird purposefully straying from the heath to defend its own cause provoked much amusement. In fact, of all the heathland birds, the Dartford warbler (*Sylvia undata*) is most tightly tied to its heathland home, ideally a stand of thick bushy gorse in the midst of matured, mainly dry, heath. The gorse thicket provides a secluded summer breeding site, from which can occasionally be heard the bird's distinctive, if plaintive, call. The gorse also provides a good source of its exclusively invertebrate diet. In a bad winter, when the surrounding heather may be snow-covered and thus unavailable for foraging, the shelter and snow-free larder that bushy gorse provides is thought to be vital to the bird's survival. Winter snow is certainly one of the major factors controlling population numbers. Another is large scale fires, when all available gorse may be uniformly burnt back to ground level, but rejuvenation of gorse is essential to the Dartford warbler, for once old and leggy gorse provides little shelter and food. In the past this regeneration was achieved by cutting gorse for fuel and possibly as a result of the controlled burns associated with heathland grazing. Thus the Dartford warbler has doubly benefited from man's activities – initially from the ground disturbance which first encouraged gorse to establish, and subsequently

TOP *A nightjar on its nest.*

LEFT *A hobby. Few falcons are more agile, and though it will take bats and small birds, its diet includes grasshoppers and dragonflies, which it can snatch and transfer to its beak without pausing in flight. Only about 150 pairs now breed in Britain, mostly in Dorset, Hampshire and Sussex.*

ABOVE *The stonechat is most at home on the uncultivated heath. It usually nests at the foot of a gorse bush, raising up to three broods if food is plentiful.*

from the treatment of it which ensured suitable bushy growth on a cyclical basis.

While Dartford warblers 'mew', nightjars are said to 'churr'. Unlike the Dartfords, nightjars are with us only in summer, when an evening walk on the heath is quite likely to be rewarded by hearing this remarkable call, and even a glimpse of the bird in flight. There is no nest as such, just a scrape on the ground – usually in a gap in the heather created by an old tree stump, or a bracken patch where the bird's mottled plumage helps provide camouflage. Feeding, mainly on moths, is concentrated at the beginning and end of the night, when the nightjar may either fly freely with wide mouth agape or conduct short sorties from a chosen perch. It is increasingly evident that nightjars are heavily dependant on habitats adjoining the heathland. These are apparently essential for feeding, but may also be used for roosting and even breeding. Nightjars have particularly benefited from the temporary areas of heathland created as conifer plantations are felled and restored.

Another ground-nester is the woodlark (*Lullula arborea*). Woodlarks seemingly like a certain amount of scrub cover in an otherwise rather open mixture of bare ground and young heather. It is not then so surprising that they are known to be particularly successful in several of the heathland sites used by the Ministry of Defence. All three of these birds, being closely linked to heathland, are all very restricted in their UK distributions, so Dorset is critical in maintaining their numbers nationally. For Dartford warblers Dorset and Hampshire are *the* critical counties in this respect.

There is nothing to equal the sight of a hobby (*Falco subbuteo*) in swift and agile pursuit of dragonflies over the heath. Another fair weather visitor, it nests in old pines towering above or around the heath, often making use of old abandoned crows' nests since it does not build its own. Although the hobby now mostly feeds over the heath rather than actually breeds upon it, the heathlands of Dorset can nevertheless also claim a key position in the national success of this rare and beautiful bird.

We cannot leave the heath without a word for the stonechat (*Saxicola torquata*), for although it does occur on other habitats in the county it is strongly associated with heathland. It also really does have the helpful habit of cheerfully displaying itself on the tops of the gorse bushes in which it feeds and breeds – unlike the Dartford warbler which is only rarely glimpsed in such an exposed position. From here its readily identifiable song, just like two stones being knocked together, can be clearly heard. Add to these attributes its colourful markings, and you understand why the stonechat is most people's favourite heathland bird. Gorse is not, of course, only important to the stonechat and Dartford warbler. Its shelter and rich invertebrate population enables a much greater diversity of birds to use the heath than would otherwise be possible. Rare and common birds alike then owe much to man's interference with the heath and the gorse which grows on it.

THE HEATH IN MODERN TIMES

Unfortunately, when John Claridge visited Dorset the way in which man interfered with the heath was already in the process of change. Only thirty years before, Isaac Taylor had produced some wonderfully detailed maps of Dorset and Hampshire showing quite plainly that the vast majority of the Poole Basin was then open heathland broken only by the more fertile soils of the main river valleys and the harbour shores – some 40,000 hectares in all. Yet less than 20 years after Claridge's visit only 30,400 remained. The losses which followed constitute one of the most relentless and dramatic habitat declines ever recorded in this country. Claridge would have been well pleased!

But not all the heathland was converted to the productive agriculture of which Claridge so approved. In the mid 1700s a few landowners started to experiment with tree planting. The first attempts with deciduous trees failed dismally on the poor soils, but pines were found to have better

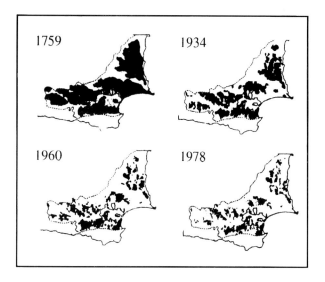

Four maps showing the reduction of the Dorset heathland between 1759 and 1978.

success. The two most commonly used were the Scots pine (*Pinus sylvestris*) and the maritime pine (*P. maritima*), the latter becoming known locally as the Bournemouth pine. Even so it was not until the formation of the Forestry Commission in 1919 that the loss of heathland to conifers commenced in earnest, this time almost exclusively with Scots pine and Corsican pine (*P. nigra*) which, alone amongst the conifers, were deemed to grow well enough to be worth the effort.

HABITAT LOSS AND FRAGMENTATION

The growth of east Dorset's towns has inevitably had a major impact on the heathlands. Poole and Christchurch expanded from small ports, while Bournemouth mushroomed out of virtually nothing to unite them and the outlying villages into one of the largest and fastest growing conurbations in the country. The original heathland is now only recalled in road names – Turbary Crescent, Bracken Road and Stonechat Close. Major new roads were required to serve the developments and both required massive supplies of raw materials. The sand and gravels which lay under the heath were suddenly in great demand and the small scale excavations of the past were replaced with extraction on an entirely different scale. Similarly the ball clay industry, which had previously

been a largely small scale enterprise, created huge pits where heathland had once been. Even as recently as the late 1970s the new oil industry took its toll as the rail terminal at Furzebrook was built on heathland. Initially the value of heathland was not understood and its conversion was widely accepted as a commendable enterprise. Later the momentum was simply too strong to stop. The overall losses fragmented and divided the habitats. The maps which document heathland loss show the progressive division of the original few major blocks into more and more fragments, increasingly separated from each other by other land uses.

Habitat loss and fragmentation has inevitably affected species, especially those with special requirements and low mobility. The population of sand lizards and smooth snakes declined drastically, with sand lizards being lost even from some sizeable surviving sites, probably as a result of widespread and repeated fires. The ladybird spider was believed lost for some time, and the natterjack toad was indeed absent until recent re-introduction. Somewhat suprisingly heathland fragments have been found to be comparatively rich in terms of numbers of species present. However, close inspection reveals that this is due to invasion of non-heathland species from surrounding habitats while characteristic heathland species are actually low in number.

DECLINE OF TRADITIONAL USE

As the Dorset heathlands were reduced and fragmented, the traditional uses of the remainder declined. Grazing became less common, eventually rare, and the pulling of bracken for bedding ceased. The arrival of the railways in the mid-nineteenth century made coal available for fuel, so that the gathering of gorse faggots, turf and peat from the heath was no longer required. Those rights of turbary, once held so precious, ceased to be exercised. At the same time the small scale mineral workings for sand, gravel and clay were replaced by mechanised extraction on a massive scale. In short, the heath had outlived its traditional function and the wildlife was left to face the consequences.

The first and most fundamental of these was that the soil nutrients were no longer continuously depleted. This permitted an unaccustomed nutrient enrichment, which in turn encouraged the growth of scrub and bracken. Without grazing or turf cutting to keep it in check, the scrub spread freely. In the decade between 1979 and 1989 the greatest loss of heathland in Dorset was to scrub. The spread of bracken was no longer checked by pulling for bedding. At the same time the heath ceased to be subject to those three factors, turf cutting, grazing and burning, which diversified its age structure, this in turn depressing the species diversity associated with structural diversity. Specialised habitats were also badly affected. New gorse sites were no longer created and existing gorse was allowed to grow leggy and unable to fulfil its key roles for invertebrates and birds. Open dry ground, so essential to many invertebrates, the sand lizard, and some birds, diminished. On the wet heath the several plants requiring the open peat created by

The expansion of Dorset's eastern towns has markedly reduced the area of heathland in the county. Alder Hills Nature Reserve is a five hectare reserve in the built-up area of Parkstone, next to a large supermarket. The combination of heath and pond makes it rich in wildlife, including a colony of sand lizards. The reserve is managed by the Dorset Wildlife Trust.

poaching by domestic stock lost their essential habitat. With the ending of peat cutting and small scale mineral working, the occurrence of ponds — home of the bladderwort, raft spider and breeding ground for so many dragonflies and damselflies — declined.

As if all this was not enough, another problem arrived from abroad. Rhododendron (*R. ponticum*) was imported from the Balkans to provide cover, where it faired exceedingly well on the acidic heathland. More recently it has been joined by the North American crowberry (*Gaultheria shallon*). Both species rapidly obliterate the heathland flora and have little to offer our native fauna in return.

In summary, the practices which had kept the heathland open, provided a diverse age structure, and created the special niches for its wildlife, came to an end, while alien and highly invasive species have ran amock. The threat which these changes posed was initially overshadowed by the more glaring problem of habitat destruction and fragmentation. However, as the deliberate destruction of the heathland has declined, these important issues have come to the fore and are as one of the two major challenges now facing heathland conservation in Dorset.

URBANISATION AND THE FUTURE

Apart from being reduced, fragmented, neglected and invaded by aliens, the heathlands of Dorset have yet another challenge to face. Many now lie in the heart of one of the most densely populated parts of the country, and none are any great distance from the Poole/Bournemouth conurbation. They are accessible to, and actively used by, the public on a significant scale. This can and does have effects upon the habitat and its wildlife.

One of the most fundamental problems arises from the structure of heather. It is low growing yet woody (ie, a dwarf shrub) and when trampled by foot, hoof or vehicle it readily snaps and dies. Thus existing paths may be easily widened and new paths created by walkers and horse riders, and when mountain or motor bikes are involved large bare scars are rapidly created. Unfortunately,

such ground cannot provide the niches required by the peat or sand loving species since they are likely to be too regularly disturbed. Indeed, they arguably present a serious hazard to some, particularly the sand lizard, who may be attracted to lay eggs in a position where they could soon be destroyed.

Another problem relates to disturbance of the fauna. Our knowledge of this subject is not as full as it should be, but there can be no doubt that some species are especially at risk. In particular the rare ground nesting birds, the nightjar and woodlark, are vulnerable to disturbance by humans and by their dogs if either wander from well-established paths. Hobbies now breed more frequently off the heath than on it and again disturbance may be a critical factor.

Finally, there is the increased risk of uncontrolled large scale burning which is now an inevitable part of the Dorset heathland scene. We have seen that in the past the heaths were probably deliberately burnt in association with grazing. However, it was small scale, carried out at a time of year when the burn was comparatively light, and conducted in an age when the heathlands were much more extensive and united. This traditional practice, therefore, gave the advantages of a diverse habitat structure, diverse flora and fauna, rejuvenated gorse and so on. At the same time it did not seriously threaten the survival of individual species, as even the less mobile generally had both the ability and time to recolonise gradually from the surrounding unburnt heath. Modest, light and infrequent fires have some advantages even today. However, the extensive, frequent and deeply burning fires to which our now reduced and fragmented heaths are all too often subjected are highly damaging. Large stands of bare and later immature heath replace the varied age structure, and less mobile species, especially the rare reptiles, are severely affected.

Undoubtedly then Dorset heathland has faced, and continues to face, significant difficulties. Direct threats have greatly diminished but not completely withdrawn, especially in respect of new roads. The consequences of ceasing traditional uses and placing the heaths within the context of urban development are considerable. However, the rarity of the habitat and the scarcity of many of the species which depend upon it clearly dictates that these difficulties must be addressed. Exactly how will be described in Chapter 8. Suffice it to say here that the efforts are directed not just at retaining existing heathland, but at restoring it through restarting or simulating those traditional uses, and at minimising the damaging influences of the urban setting. Efforts are also required to extend and relink the heathlands. Through such enterprise the wildlife of the Dorset heathlands should be available to delight the eyes of anybody prepared simply to really open their eyes and look.

The Dorset heath at Studland, looking towards the Agglestone.

FOUR

DOWNLANDS AND MEADOWS

A BYGONE AGE

Of all the habitats now valued for nature conservation there is probably none more evocative of a bygone age – a time of plenty for wildlife – than grasslands. True that marvellous old woods and rare expanses of heath are also windows into the past, but maybe it is because grassland of one form or another is still abundant, albeit of minimal nature conservation value, that we can so readily see the scale of what has gone.

The tiny fragments of grassland still rich in herbs and grasses, whether on limestone or acid, neutral, wet or dry soils, are but a minute proportion of what once existed, even in a county like Dorset. The losses are quite recent. Many of us can recall, increasingly distantly, childhood memories of flowery meadows, turned to sweet-smelling hay stacks in high summer; or aromatic, springy downland turf humming with insects, and fascinating damp hollows sparkling with kingcups and milkmaids in spring. We can still go to places, treasured sites perhaps in favourite nature reserves, where all of these are still to be found. But our annual pilgrimages to see the cowslips or the blue butterflies probably mean passing mile upon mile of re-seeded blue-green leys or permanent pastures burgeoning with grass responding to fertiliser, to the exclusion of most flowers. Until quite recently many of these fields would

Cowslips and early purple orchids on the slopes of Hambledon Hill.

have held the same turf that we now have to travel miles to see.

It is only since the massive and cheap availability of inorganic fertilisers and the armoury of chemicals to eradicate weeds and pests that the major changes to grasslands have happened. Before the Second World War, grasslands would have of course been ploughed, but reversion occurred quite readily, without the chemical applications of today. Many old grasslands, too difficult or poor to plough, would have been traditionally cut for hay or grazed, producing less of a crop and maintaining fewer livestock. Only in the last 50 years has the declining quality of our grasslands become so evident and, perhaps worse, so irreversible.

Much is rightly made of ancient habitats. What has taken centuries, even millenia to evolve, cannot be replaced with ease once lost. We should think of such sites – an ancient forest with veteran trees or the wind-blown turf of an Iron Age hillfort – with no less awe and wonder than we routinely feel for more recent, man-made treasures such as medieval cathedrals or great works of art. With grasslands of nature conservation value, age is not the only important factor, however. Such sites can have high interest even if the turf may have been broken in the past. The hillforts, celtic fields, strip lynchets, trackways and more recent cultivations have often reverted to grasslands of outstanding nature conservation importance today. The critical factor is whether the soils have been modified and the nutrient status increased.

Compared with heathlands on free-draining sandy soils, grasslands have usually developed over more water retentive soils with at least some clay fraction. Nutrients like phosphates bind readily to the clay particles and do not easily leach from the soil. A fertiliser application can thus substantially alter the balance of the soil chemistry; and the higher nutrient level favours the few demanding species like certain grasses, that dominate and crowd out the original mix of perhaps 30 or 40 wild grasses and herbs. Repeated a few times and backed up with weedkillers, the original vegetation is effectively lost. Such has been the fate of most of our herb-rich grasslands.

The view north-west from Shipton Hill, near Bridport, across the rolling mixture of arable land and pasture in west Dorset. The medieval strip lynchets near Uploders are clearly etched on the hillside beyond the main Bridport to Dorchester road, and Lewesdon Hill can be seen on the left hand horizon. Despite the image of Dorset as a largely agricultural county, grasslands with a high conservation value are now scarce.

In 1984 the then Nature Conservancy Council estimated that 95% of all grassland in Great Britain had lost its nature conservation value. Much of that loss will have happened in the past 50 years.

Grassland would once have been naturally rare. In the time of the wild-wood, before our Stone Age ancestors started to make an impact and began the forest clearance to farm stock and crops, what we now take for granted as the classic English patchwork of fields, had not emerged. Maybe only at the extremes of exposure on the loftiest, bleakest sites, or strongly influenced by the sea, was there any open habitat suitable for grassland species. In Dorset it is perhaps easiest to envisage this on newly formed features such as sand or shingle beaches and river or sea cliffs kept free from trees through natural erosion. The periodic landslips that have formed the great under-cliffs of our county, such as at White Nothe, Worbarrow Bay, Golden Cap and Lyme will have swept away woody species every so often and provided open conditions where today's grassland plants and animals could maintain a toehold. Then as the effects of tree clearance, cultivation and grazing of both wild and domestic stock had their effect, the wonderful range of grasslands started to evolve. Over many centuries, in response to different soils and under a continuous pattern of use – of grazing or regular cutting or deliberate flooding – our grasslands developed.

Like heathland, grassland is often called man-made, but this is to credit humans with a skill and an intention beyond their ability. Bronze Age man did not set out with a vision of the heathland landscape as his goal, nor did the stone and iron-tooled tribes of the chalk hills mix wildflower and grass seed to create meadow or downland turf. The grassland we see today, where it has not been transformed by modern agriculture, is the result of nature's response to centuries of a constant management influence – grazing or cutting – on the particular local conditions of soil and climate. Thus, on the chalk uplands, from Eggardon Hill in the south-west, across our county and as far away as the Yorkshire Wolds, downland turf of a broadly similar character evolved. On the heavier, more fertile clay soils of every English county, pastures of a similar floral composition have developed.

No-one planted the wild thyme and clustered bellflowers; the green-winged orchids and spring sedge; the quaking grass or meadow oat. These and many other herbs, grasses and sedges are the constant components of different grassland sites on comparable soils with the same long history of management influence, the length and breadth of the country. To add to a fascinating constancy that would defeat even the most sophisticated modern habitat re-creation project, there is the subtle variation we find across the range of sites. So in the drier, hotter south-east, the chalk is classically orchid-rich. At its western limit in Dorset where rainfall is significantly more, there are naturally fewer orchids but the abundance of devil's-bit scabious, betony and rough hawkbit are striking character features. More locally still such differences are apparent. On the chalk of north-east Dorset, extending to our neighbouring counties of north-west Hampshire and south Wiltshire, the nationally scarce dwarf sedge is locally abundant on suitable sites, but nowhere else, even though apparently suitable chalk grassland sites still occur to the east and west.

CONSERVING GRASSLANDS

These are puzzles, perhaps to solve and certainly to marvel at. They take the richness and fascination of this plant community far beyond the dry inquiry – what orchids does it have? Indeed because herb-rich grassland was abundant not so long ago in every county, the number of really rare species is limited. Even rapidly declining species like green-winged orchid were widespread if local. This has made a realisation of the plight of surviving rich grassland and its defence even more difficult.

Dorset's herb-rich downlands and meadows are now home to a wide range of flora and fauna.

TOP LEFT *Betony, one of the flowers of the chalk and limestone turf.*

TOP RIGHT *A meadow pipit, easily recognized by its sharp call-note.*

ABOVE *A field vole, whose diet of plants, fruits, nuts and fungi make it as much at home in hedgerows and banks as in lowland pasture.*

RIGHT *Chalkhill and common blue butterflies sunning themselves.*

Cowslips in flower on the slopes of Fontmell Down Nature Reserve. Only regular grazing or cutting will stop scrub and gorse establishing themselves on the steeper slopes.

The scarcity of heathland is matched by its impressive list of nationally rare species. This has been used to good effect to convince the nature conservation bodies to commit lean resources to saving the habitat, and in persuading planners and public inquiry inspectors that here is something unique that should not be built on. For grassland it is much harder, when the plant atlas suggests that most of the component species are widespread. There is a critical role for recorders to maintain up-to-date information on the number and location of all surviving grassland fragments, and for all naturalists to appreciate the scarcity and vulnerability of what is left and promote its active conservation with fervour.

In Dorset the recording is in good hands, with excellent recent information maintained by the Dorset Environmental Records Centre, to supplement earlier surveys of different grassland types. Grassland of nature conservation value is now more adequately reflected in protected sites throughout the county. Conservation ownership and management of grassland sites has also increased in recent years.

We have in Dorset approximately 5000 hectares of grassland with a high conservation value. Half of the grassland sites of Special Scientific Interest are on chalk and limestone. These tend to be of a larger size than the remaining neutral and acid grassland areas, which in many cases have become fragmented.

The National Trust has continued to acquire important grassland on chalk, limestone and clay, especially near the coast, but the acquisitions have also been inland, as the impressive continuous tract of downland at Fontmell and Melbury Downs south of Shaftesbury illustrates. There are now National Nature Reserves on chalk grassland at Hambledon Hill and at Hogcliff near Maiden Newton, with a new designation expected for the

Valley of Stones. The Dorset Wildlife Trust's own portfolio of important grasslands continues to expand, with small but very rich sites at Corfe Mullen and Bracketts Coppice following the inspirational acquisition of unimproved farmland at Lower Kingcombe Farm in west Dorset. That bold move in 1987 caught the imagination of the nature conservation world and, as well as safeguarding the largest tract of traditionally managed neutral grassland surviving in Dorset, doubtless inspired other Wildlife Trusts to follow suit.

Whilst ownership by a nature conservation body may often be of critical importance, especially to save a site from certain change, many grassland fragments will continue to remain in private hands. Whatever the ownership the survival of grassland for wildlife will depend on continuing favourable management. The days of massive reclamation with grants to do it are probably gone for ever. Perhaps the biggest threat today is neglect. Without annual grazing or cutting and removal of the year's crop of herbage, the grassland quickly becomes rank and dominated by a few coarse species like tall oat or cocksfoot. Imagine the lawn left for a few seasons without the routine mowing! The great number of smaller, less aggressive species including almost all of the typical herbs of interesting grassland are quickly suppressed. After a few years they may not even survive in the seed bank in the soil. The tendency for scrub and trees to take over is also clear. Bramble or gorse usually establish first, but trees are equally quick in taking advantage of the lack of cropping, so that in a few years a thicket and eventually a new wood emerge.

There is a tension here for nature conservation. Surely trees are good and we need more, not fewer? But the secondary woodland that would grow if left to its own devices is no substitute for the richness of ancient woodland, rightly as a habitat of outstanding value, and the grassland lost to scrub and trees would be a serious further loss of an already scarce and depleted natural resource. Positive intervention for nature conservation, by cutting scrub and keeping a grazing or cutting system in place, can maintain the balance. The big threat comes when the grassland fragment no longer plays its traditional role in the farming system. We must have all seen isolated steep downland banks, once part of an extensive grazing pattern, but now islands in arable land. No animals can reach the bank to graze; indeed the farm possibly no longer has any stock. The grass bank is doomed and often as not its fate is further sealed by deliberate tree planting.

Even some conservation sites have suffered such a loss, for fear that cutting or grazing of the flowers would stop the treasured objects setting seed. However, grassland has been managed by summer grazing and cutting for centuries. Grassland herbs and grasses are adapted to this regime; indeed they depend on it. Most of the component species are perennials that do not need annual recruitment from seed, and in any case most will manage to set seed from a late flowering or from the many individual plants that don't get cropped. We can see only too well that road verges long protected from their routine cut, change often to coarse grass and cow parsley.

TYPES OF GRASSLAND

CHALK GRASSLAND

Though grassland worthy of conservation is today very limited, both in Dorset and nationally, there are various types with different characteristic species. Most plentiful in Dorset is grassland that has developed over chalk and limestone soils. The great swathe of chalk country that strikes a diagonal band south-west to north-east across the county, with a narrow tail across the south, forms the familiar Dorset Downs and Purbeck Hills. It carries on north, through Cranborne Chase, into Hampshire and Wiltshire, splitting into the North and South Downs and the Chilterns, all with their fragments of surviving chalk downland. The narrow southern limb forms the spine of the Isle of Wight, whose chalk cliffs of Tennyson Down and the Needles can be glimpsed from Ballard Cliff and Old Harry rocks, their immediate counterpart in our county.

From the concentration of ancient earthworks on the chalk downs we can suppose that this landscape was amongst the first to emerge as the original forest of the wild-wood was cleared. Perhaps the commanding positions and possibly the thinner more easily worked soil and correspondingly less vigorous trees made the downland heights especially attractive to our early forebears. We are left today with the still awe-inspiring remains of their settlements; but the scale of clearance to make the hillforts and camps must have extended well beyond their present bounds. The ramparts that we see today would have been revetted with timber, consuming thousands of trees, probably from managed woodland such as coppice. Stand on the heights of Hambledon Hill, and imagine its tiered banks lined with paling, and the scale of the work and its impact on the surrounding land starts to emerge. Originally such ramparts were bare, gleaming chalk, but in the millenia that have passed, turf has developed over the banks. It is often these steep, drained, thin-soiled banks that support the best surviving herb-rich turf.

There is evidence that some chalk plants only occur on this most ancient of turf, in existence for perhaps 3000 years or more and never ploughed. Such rarities in Dorset include burnt-tip orchid, hovering on the eastern county boundary, on the massive Bokerly Dyke, and field fleawort on earthworks, as on Hod Hill. Some plants though, despite a reputation for lack of colonising ability, clearly can move into more recent grassland. Bee orchid for instance is not uncommon in the turf that has grown over old quarries, or even shell holes in the Army Ranges. Even early spider orchid, though usually a component of old turf, can flourish in the more recent grassland of abandoned quarries. Yet other chalk herbs occur only where the turf has been disturbed and so are not regular components of the ancient turf. Such early colonists include kidney vetch and the two

Burnt-tip orchids retain a tenuous hold in Dorset on Bokerly Dyke, close to the eastern county boundary.

The bee orchid, a rare plant of chalky soils found in grassy places and along the edge of woods.

The skylark's song is one the most evocative sounds of the downland. It sings to attract females and defend its territory, and is the only British bird that can sing when hovering, descending, and rising almost vertically from the ground.

frequent umbellifers of chalky soils, wild carrot and wild parsnip.

The theme of rich turf surviving only on steep ground is repeated away from the hillfort earthworks. In general only the steepest natural downland slopes still carry flowery grassland. The ancient sheepwalks that stretched across countless thousands of acres of the southern chalk have long since gone to the plough and much now grows cereals. The pattern is easily seen in Dorset on the gentle slopes of the broad dip slope of the chalk, rising gradually from the heathland basin. Almost no chalk grassland survives here. It is not until there is a valley with steeper sides cutting into this landscape, or the scarp slope plunges away to the vales around the outer edges of the chalk massif, that the more substantial chalk grassland fragments appear. On the steep slopes of the Purbeck Hills are remnants of surviving turf.

The local concentrations of good chalk grassland, rich in flowers and often insects too, tend then to follow the outer, higher and steeper margins of the chalk. The Purbeck Ridge, which reaches the coast in spectacular switchback plunges between Flowers Barrow and White Nothe, is one such spot. Some of the valley sides of rivers like the Cerne and Sydling and other tributaries of the Frome and Stour provide surviving slopes. The scarp slope itself, especially at its extremities, as at Melbury Down in the north and Eggardon and Haydon in the west, is another area where chalk grassland has survived.

Very little unimproved grassland remains on the flatter chalk since almost always this has been available for cultivation. Only where this has been prevented for some reason do we get a hint of such a landscape. Part of Bindon Range behind Lulworth still has gently rolling chalk grassland, like a little piece of Salisbury Plain transposed, and the western end of the Purbeck Ridge top, between Whiteway Hill and Flowers Barrow, and the top of Bindon Hill itself, have rare examples of hilltop turf. Elsewhere such flat surfaces have been ploughed and even where they have been put back to grassland, the turf has little of its original character. It is interesting but perhaps not surprising that these examples are all within Ministry of Defence land, where agricultural progress has been frozen since the 1940s.

The chalk outcrop is the most obvious area of calcareous soils, and thus it is here that most chalk grassland survives in Dorset. But there are other areas with calcareous rock and these also can support fine, herb-rich turf. The most concentrated and well-known of the limestone areas in Dorset is in the extreme south, forming the Isle of Portland and part of the Purbeck coast, between Swanage and St Aldhelm's Head. Here the Purbeck and Portland limestones form not only the spectacular cliff coast but underlie much of the nearby land. Wherever this survives as grassland, and especially in the long sweep from Durlston to Worth Matravers, 'chalk' grassland can be found, but it is not all ancient. The clear and striking marks of earlier cultivations are evident near Worth and Seacombe with wonderful tiers of medieval lynchet banks, and more recent quarries here and on Portland have regrown some excellent herb-rich turf. The common factors are thin, lime-rich soils, unaffected by fertilisers. Many of the components of grassland on the chalk are present here on the limestone, but there are some differences too.

There are outcrops of limestone elsewhere in Dorset, but less extensively. Little fragments of 'chalk' turf can sometimes be found, indicating limestone soils, where agricultural improvement has not completely altered the grassland. The narrow limestone band north of Weymouth has such examples, as does the odd larger site — like Chalbury Hill. Further inland pockets of the Inferior Oolite can be traced with revealing turf, as near Powerstock Castle and around Sherborne.

PLANTS OF CHALK AND LIMESTONE

Whilst there is a strong common thread running through all calcareous grassland, with many species present throughout, there are also differences. Perhaps because the limestones are often harder, but also because they are often covered by a deeper clay-rich soil than much of the chalk, the calcareous influence can be less marked. The turf over the Dorset limestones, especially those outcrops away from the coast, has some similarities with neutral grassland and perhaps only the more obvious chalk indicator plants are frequent. Wherever herbs like salad burnet, hoary plantain and stemless thistle occur there is some calcareous influence. On dry grassland sites the presence of glaucous sedge, quaking grass, wild thyme and common bird's-foot-trefoil can be expected and though not confined to chalk and limestone, they are frequent here. Then there is a long list of more exacting chalk herbs and mosses, scarcely found away from these soils. Such gems as small scabious, horseshoe vetch, common rock-rose and clustered bellflower are typical of this select group, along with a number of rarer species, found perhaps only on a handful of sites.

Clustered bellflower, an attractive flower of Dorset's chalk and limestone downland turf.

We all have our favourite downland flowers, perhaps evoking a memory of a site from early botanising days; seeing such plants is like meeting old friends again. Many of us will be content to note these individual species; others may go further and make a list of all plants present, including the grasses and mosses. If this is done on a range of sites it may be possible to notice that there are several fairly distinct plant communities, even within the category of chalk grassland.

The most widespread of these associations, representing classic chalk and limestone grassland, is herb-rich turf with many species of fine-leaved grasses and rosette-forming herbs, in which no single species dominates. Indeed this is the famous turf in which it is not uncommon to find upwards of 25 different species within a single metre square. Some of those plants listed above will be joined by squinancy-wort, sheep's-fescue, meadow oat-grass, lady's bedstraw, burnet saxifrage and autumn gentian — with added spice provided by less widespread plants like early gentian, hairy rock-cress, chalk milkwort and, if you look really carefully, bastard-toadflax.

This classic chalk turf has a variant that is particularly well shown in Dorset, and which is especially conspicuous in late summer when the blue and purple of many of the flowers creates a distinctive and attractive haze over the downland. Most of the regular flowers and grasses are there, but devil's-bit and small scabious, betony, saw-wort, clustered bellflower and ox-eye daisy are notably frequent. The strikingly western distribution of this grouping on the English chalk and limestone is perhaps a reflection of the wetter conditions, especially in winter, together with the warm summer conditions typical of southern localities. The higher incidence of traditional cattle grazing on the downs in Dorset may also be significant in the evolution of this beautiful grassland.

Within these variations of classic chalk turf, plants and their dependant insects show their locational preferences. The typical devil's-bit/betony turf is especially linked to west and south-west facing slopes. Horseshoe-vetch and perhaps rockrose, however, are most often found on south facing slopes. The north and east facing downs may have fewer herbs, though cowslip and pignut are often more plentiful and the turf is often richer in mosses, less prone to drying out on these moister slopes. The seasons bring their changes too. In earlier summer it is the time of vetches, and splashes of bright yellow bird's-foot-trefoil and horseshoe vetch contrast with the blue and pink of milkworts. The unusual combination of cowslips and early purple orchids is another attractive local feature of some of our downs.

Another fairly distinctive association of chalk and limestone flora, again very typical of western Britain is that of short, tussocky turf with sheep's-fescue the main grass, found around outcrops of the hardest chalk and limestone rock. This community can be found where rock breaks through the normal turf, on bluffs and clifftops: in Dorset the coastal limestone and hard chalk of the Purbeck Ridge are its home. Other characteristic plants are carline thistle, wild thyme, mouse-ear and yellow-wort, with occasionally the rare early gentian in early summer, as along the sparse clifftop vegetation of Ballard Cliff.

The coastal chalk and limestone are also the main home in Dorset of another plant community in which the coarse tor grass is dominant. Much maligned and even feared by chalk grassland managers, tor grass turf is, in fact, of very restricted distribution in Britain. Its bad reputation stems from the rank nature of the turf when ungrazed, often to the exclusion of most typical chalk herbs. When well-managed, however, tor grass turf can be almost as rich as classic chalk grassland, though there are plenty of examples of its less appealing form. The limestone of Purbeck and the sweep of chalk across the south of Dorset are its main locations, though small patches prosper on a few inland sites.

Ungrazed, this turf has few component species able to compete with the tall, coarse grass. Glaucous sedge, stinking iris and wood-sage can persist under such conditions, but when the turf is properly grazed there are plenty of attractive herbs and grasses. Perhaps foremost among these is the early spider orchid, in Dorset only found in tor grass turf on Purbeck's limestone. One of the localities for this intriguing plant, indeed its only spot away from the coastal slope, is Townsend Nature Reserve near Swanage. In the early 1980s this was a mass of deep tor grass, with only the steep banks and mounds of the former quarry still carrying short, open turf. The prospect of trying to control tor grass by cutting and removing material seemed impossibly daunting for the Wildlife Trust. Then the opportunity to graze with a couple of horses came along, transforming the site. This exercise in the value of horse grazing as an aid to management was used later by the National Trust on its Spyway and Seacombe property in Purbeck, where Exmoor ponies have brought the extensive limestone grassland back into good condition after a spell of relying on sheep. So for tor grass turf, grazing by older horses or cattle is the answer; sheep are useless! Where a thatch of old grass has developed an initial burn may help so long as this is small in scale and is followed by appropriate grazing.

In its most extreme coastal localities tor grass turf can retain its diversity even without grazing. Perhaps exposure to wind, salt and sun is influential, with the added bonus of the thatch of dead leaves so typical of ungrazed sites being blown away from these coastal slopes. This taller but still diverse turf can be seen between White Nothe and Bat's Head, and again on the descent from Gad Cliff to Worbarrow Bay. Saw-wort seems to be particularly prominent in the sward in such places and pyramidal orchid is also quite frequent.

A further restricted grassland type occurs on our calcareous soils, again with a coarse grass dominating. Upright brome is the key species, and this is rather like tor grass in its unpalatable qualities. There are only small areas of this turf in Dorset – on the Isle of Portland, scattered across Purbeck, and in some spots on the northern inland chalk.

Within many of the chalk and limestone sites there are often pockets of grassland of slightly different character, in which yet another range of plants can grow. In the bottom of dry valleys, at the foot of the steep downs and also in the hollows between ancient earthworks, a deeper soil has usually accumulated, encouraging a wider range of plants to appear. One of the most noticeable is the delicate meadow saxifrage that adorns parts of the hilltop at Hambledon. Anthills are a feature of many old grassland sites free from recent ploughing, including downland. Again, due to the industry of their builders, yellow meadow ants, these hummocks present sifted, free-draining soils with somewhat different properties from the surrounding grassland. More diminutive plants can often grow here amongst the fine grass, and these may include concentrations of mouse-ear, wild thyme and early whitlow grass. An attractive local moss *Rhodobryum roseum* occurs only in this habitat on a few downland sites.

NEUTRAL GRASSLAND

There is no absolute cut-off point between the different grassland types. Elements of the flora of chalk or limestone soils will continue into pastures over other rock types that have a calcareous influence. Thus clay soils on the Fuller's Earth, Forest Marble and some of the other Dorset Jurassic rocks can support neutral grassland in which a few familiar chalk plants still occur. At the other end of the spectrum there is a gradation from acid grassland into full-scale heathland or mire, seen most clearly perhaps over the Greensand soils and on some sites on the Tertiary clays around the margins of the heathland basin in south-east Dorset. But in its typical form neutral grassland is distinctive, attractive – and sadly now scarce.

Only some 1400 hectares of herb-rich neutral grassland remains in Dorset today and much of this is in small fragments, even single fields or parts of fields. Nonetheless it is widely, if very thinly, scattered, since until perhaps 50 years ago such grassland was common in most parishes, wherever clay soils occur. Fine sites are still left

ABOVE *Dyer's greenweed.*

LEFT *Green-winged orchids in the Dorset Wildlife Trust's meadow reserve at Corfe Mullen.*

OPPOSITE PAGE *Buttercups and clovers in the old hay meadow Lady's Mead at Kingcombe Meadows. The 152 hectare nature reserve is owned by the Dorset Wildlife Trust.*

then across the county, from a cluster of small fields near Shaftesbury in the north to a few pockets along the coast in the south; from Wootton and Lyme in the west across to the Avon valley in the east. Such fields of neutral grassland will be managed as permanent pasture, typically with cattle grazing, and in some cases as traditional hay fields with or without grazing in late summer, after the hay cut. The particular management, as well as the soil type and its wetness will affect the components of the turf and no two sites are the same, but there is a consistent character.

A range of grasses forms the turf, with no single species dominating. Typically perennial rye-grass, the ubiquitous component of agriculturally improved grassland, is present at only low level. Crested dog's-tail, red fescue, Yorkshire fog, common bent and sweet-vernal grass are all frequent, and in some sites quaking grass, heath-grass and the attractive meadow barley may also

occur. Sedges are much more varied and frequent than on the chalk, with glaucous sedge, spring sedge, carnation sedge, oval sedge and hairy sedge all common, perhaps joined on a few rich sites, at the wetter end of the range, by flea sedge and tawny sedge.

Many herbs occur in the best examples of neutral grassland, creating an attractive and colourful sward. Lesser knapweed, ox-eye daisy, clovers, dandelion, meadow vetchling and buttercups are bold and obvious components but a large number of other herbs can occur, some of them much less common. Lady's bedstraw, yarrow and agrimony are most frequent in those pastures with a more calcareous influence, whilst the attractive mix of devil's-bit, betony, tormentil and pignut probably reflects a slightly more acidic tendency. In the best sites there will be one or more of several much less frequent plants, such as lady's mantle, adder's-tongue fern, pepper-saxifrage, dyer's greenweed and that Dorset speciality, corky-fruited water dropwort – a herb only found in this country in central southern England, with Dorset the centre of its distribution. It appears to survive some agricultural improvement so can sometimes persist in otherwise uninteresting grassland, and is a regular component of the best of Dorset's surviving meadows and pastures.

Also typical of the best neutral grasslands, though sadly scarce in Dorset, is green-winged orchid. There are now few fields with this quietly handsome flower in profusion, but the Dorset Wildlife Trust's new nature reserve at Corfe Mullen has saved one such traditional meadow. At the opposite end of the county, at Wootton Fitzpaine, there is a small group of fine fields where wild daffodils still flower, to be followed by a scattering of green-winged orchids throughout the herb-rich turf.

Most of the plants will occur whether the grass is grazed or cut for hay. Yellow-rattle is more fussy. As an annual, the distribution of its early ripening seeds is much helped by hay-making. Its semi-parasitic habit can under some circumstances locally weaken the vigour of the grasses in the sward, thus reducing the hay crop. Grazing hinders the distribution of its seed, so a season of grazing rather than hay-making is usually enough to restore the balance.

While the sward may be of fairly even composition throughout these few precious neutral grassland meadows and pastures, damper features can add to the diversity. This is most obvious where springs emerge or cause water to approach the surface in flushes, often where the underlying geology changes. An examination of the older 2½" O.S. maps will reveal a fairly widespread use of marsh symbols, but often as not a field visit now will show little trace of the feature they once symbolised, or the additional species they encouraged. Not many have survived drainage and reclamation but where they have, they are exciting sites indeed.

A transition from relatively free-draining soils to more impeded drainage may give rise to springs or flushes. A classic occurrence of this is where the greensand is underlain by heavier clays. Some of the small fields between Morcombelake and the coast, and the Toller/Kingcombe area, show this feature well. At Kingcombe the valley of the River Hooke cuts through the slightly base-rich Fuller's Earth and this underlies the bottom of the saucer. The higher, outer edges of the vale are formed by Greensand, over a narrow band of impervious Gault Clay. This feature occurs on the north and south sides of the valley, but on the north side the greensand itself is overlain by chalk, a variation reflected in the character of the grassland and the flushes that occur.

Walking south from the Dorset Wildlife

Yellow-flowering petty whin flourishes in Lower South Mead at Kingcombe. The transition from free-draining acid soils to more impeded drainage creates springs or flushes, which suit this plant.

Trust nature reserve base at Pound Cottage, Kingcombe, the first few fields are rich neutral grassland, with such gems as lady's mantle and corky-fruited water dropwort amongst the many other flowers. The flush line is encountered at about mid-slope and has small mires that have a different vegetation from the fields. Purple moor-grass, bent grasses and sphagnum mosses dominate the wettest areas, often with abundant marsh violet, here the food plant of the increasingly scarce small pearl-bordered fritillary butterfly. Marsh pennywort, meadow thistle, lousewort, heath-spotted orchid and petty whin, uncommon in Dorset, occur in the damp sward around these flushes and the rushes here are soft rush and jointed rush. All of these indicate acidic conditions, and this is further confirmed by the local occurrence of cross-leaved heath.

A similar walk north from Pound Cottage will lead to Mary Well and the flushed field above Mary Well Withy Bed. There is little sign here of any of the flush vegetation of the south side of the valley. Instead the wet turf has hard rush, meadowsweet, ragged robin, giant horsetail and the occasional common-spotted or marsh orchid. On this side of the valley, water drains through a capping of chalk as well as greensand, before meeting the clay; on the south side rain falls directly onto the greensand soils and unlike the chalk, these are acidic. With the wet features in neutral grassland then, their character is often more influenced by overlying than underlying geology.

The flushes and especially the base-rich fens that still survive around the edges of the chalk outcrop in west Dorset are rich not only for their plants; a handful of such sites support a diverse community of invertebrates including several nationally scarce species. Craneflies, snail-killing flies, soldier flies, leaf beetles, soldier beetles and weevils are among the scarce insects, and spiders and snails also contribute to the rich mix of largely unnoticed wildlife in these fascinating and usually small-scale habitats of grassland and fen.

Damp rather than very wet pastures with an abundance of devil's-bit are the traditional habitat of one of our most rapidly declining butterflies, the marsh fritillary. This still thrives in a few such marshy fields in Dorset and one of the colonies, in a superb fragment of surviving old grass and fen in the Blackmore Vale, is of a size to be of national significance. Rather oddly, marsh fritillary is also found on a few of the Dorset chalk downland sites where its foodplant is common and the turf is grazed appropriately by cattle.

There is often a gradation of neutral grassland into wetter fen conditions. Great mounds of tussock sedge stride across such sites and sometimes in the valley bottom, a strip of alder or sallow carr occurs. The best ones have remained open with cattle grazing. Within its acre or so of herb-rich turf at least 14 different sedge species can be found in one field at Kingcombe. Other interesting plants of these fenny, peaty sites include water avens, marsh valerian, early marsh orchid and very occasionally marsh helleborine. Several local mosses occur typically in these restricted and now precious sites.

A high water table, even seasonal flooding, together with base-rich water provides the conditions for another type of neutral grassland now rare in Dorset. This is the turf of the flat flood plains of the chalk streams, like the Frome and Piddle and their tributaries. Here the combination of naturally productive soil and an abundant supply of constant relatively warm and rich water was once used to construct water meadows. At its peak some 200 years ago, this grassland management depended on taking water from the chalk river in leats, to feed channels on slight ridges across the fields, and allowing this water to trickle across the turf, draining off in the gulleys and back to the river. This flush of warm, rich water encouraged an early bite of spring grass, providing a valuable and timely supplement to the feeding of the huge flocks of sheep pastured across the downland landscape of southern England in the seventeenth and eighteenth centuries.

The grassland was carefully managed, even hand-weeded to remove coarser and less palatable species, including many herbs, so a turf dominated by grass resulted. No examples of this water meadow system are now worked in Dorset, though the valley flood plains still bear many traces of the sluices, carriers and the slightly ridged surface so characteristic of this ingenious land use. These can be easily spotted from the roads across the Frome valley at Dorchester for instance. Even though permanent pasture sometimes remains, the level ground and natural productivity have meant that almost without exception the grassland has been improved by

The marsh fritillary butterfly is declining rapidly, but a few colonies still thrive in a handful of sites in Dorset.

Winter flooding on the water meadows of Wareham Common.

herbicides and fertilisers, even if ploughing has not occurred. A few examples have been partly abandoned and now support rich fen vegetation, and one or two examples survive of the grassland type that probably preceded the water meadow management throughout many of our valleys.

On part of Wareham Common can be seen an area of turf beside the lower Piddle that stays wet in spring after winter flooding and which, for a few brief days, boasts an unusual abundance of marsh marigolds in the sward. Several grasses comprise the turf with a number of other herbs, like lady's smock and ragged robin, together with the frequent presence of the inconspicuous, creeping brown sedge. The site is grazed by cattle and horses, completing a portrait probably typical of the grassland that once extended over much of the flood plains of the chalk rivers, away from acidic drainage from the heaths, before such water meadows were intensively managed or 'improved' by modern agriculture. There are only tiny fragments of this type of neutral grassland left and the few acres at Wareham Common, not consumed by the by-pass, are probably the largest such area in Dorset.

ACID GRASSLAND

There is even less grassland worthy of conserving on acidic soils in Dorset than survives on neutral soils. This has probably always been the case, since markedly acidic soils are rather more limited in extent than the great bands of broadly neutral clay soils that once supported herb-rich turf. Many of the acid soils are poor and free-draining, or in contrast totally water-logged, and only able to support heather-dominated heathland or mire. These internationally renowned communities have been described in the previous chapter.

Where the conditions are not so extreme, or where there has been a history of grazing, acid grassland communities do still grow, sometimes as a gradation from dwarf-shrub heath; sometimes on the edges of mires and flushes, and sometimes as a distinct but usually localised grassland type. The main areas in Dorset are thus the acidic soils of the heathland basin in the south-east and the greensand hilltops typical of west Dorset. But locally patches of clay-with-flints on the top of some of the chalk downs can support pockets of heathy grassland. The same is true of the Bridport Sands, such as in the wonderfully sinuous valleys south of Poorton. Here the steep slopes have made cultivation impossible, encouraging a species-poor turf of acid grassland.

Perhaps because these acid grasslands tend to have less diversity they have been seen as poor examples of heathland, or semi-improved neutral pasture, and until recently their conservation has been largely ignored, but the best of them are amongst the most exciting for scarce species of any of our grasslands. Typically, the turf's main grasses will be sheep's fescue and common bent, with others like sweet-vernal grass and Yorkshire fog also frequent. Sheep's sorrel is abundant, especially on the drier sites prone to drought, perhaps with heath bedstraw, pill sedge, green-ribbed sedge and field woodrush. In general, agricultural improvement has been the main cause of loss, but, in south-east Dorset, the lack of heathland grazing has allowed coarse vegetation and scrub to thrive at the expense of the finer turf. In a rare surviving example of grazed turf, bordering heathland, there is a clutch of scarce species, including smooth cat's-ear, clustered and subterranean clovers, pale dog-violet and mossy stonecrop. The resumption of grazing on a number of the Dorset heaths may allow this rich medley of plants to flourish again.

On acid hilltops, on the downs and greensand, heathy grassland which includes heathers and bilberry may still be found, together with many of the grasses and herbs of acid turf. Bristle-bent grass, purple moor-grass and wavy hair-grass also thrive, the latter only in the west of Dorset since it is strangely absent from the main heathland area of the south-east. Such acidic patches are often small, giving way within a few paces to chalk grassland, as at the Valley of Stones and near Flower's Barrow. In a few other spots, localised screes of leached chalk and flint pebbles occur, again with an acid grassland character and often with typical heathland lichens and mosses. Melbury Down in the north of the county has some fine examples of this unusual community.

The most extensive acid grassland site in Dorset, and probably one of the finest in the country, is Corfe Common, a remarkable working common dotted with tumuli and the later hollow-ways, formed during Corfe's heyday at the heart of the medieval stone trade in Purbeck. The long continuous history of cattle and pony grazing, and its location on the mildly acidic wealden sands and clays, are the keys to Corfe Common's richness. To these must be added the frequent occurrence of springs and flushes, all of them combining to create a habitat remarkable for numerous plants and several very scarce insects. Masses of wild chamomile; acres of saw-wort, betony and devil's-

Blackthorn in flower on Corfe Common, with Kingston on the skyline.

bit; heath, marsh and spotted orchids; bog pimpernel and pale butterwort; adder's-tongue and bitter vetch — these and many, many other gems abound on the Common. Happily, their future seems secure now that the National Trust is maintaining the vital grazing and tackling invading scrub and bracken. Some of the original Common was reclaimed in the Second World War and has remained as improved grassland. The Trust is slowly restoring it, a task that takes time. This can best be seen on the few acres that were ploughed in wartime and returned to Common management after the war. Even now, though within exactly the same grazing regime, it lacks several of the herbs so abundant in the undamaged turf alongside.

Corfe Common has both wet and dry acid grassland. There are interesting elements of wet acid communities, often in intimate mixtures with other grassland types, in some of our river valleys, where the influence of acidic drainage from the heaths meets the base-rich water of the chalk streams. Good examples of this occur at Wareham Common, the Moors and at Tadnoll. Frequent components of the turf in such sites are purple-moor grass, lousewort and meadow thistle, together with several sedges and jointed rush. Bottle sedge, marsh cinquefoil and bog-bean are typical along the ditch edges, while very locally greater burnet and whorled caraway may be found. It is in one of the two places where whorled caraway can be seen that viper's-grass grows in its only locality in England.

So our grasslands have their share of nationally rare and scarce species, but most interesting is the range of grassland communities that exist, each reflecting some subtle change in soils, ground water and past management. Sadly, even now the few remaining hectares of unspoiled grassland remain under threat, but the great upsurge in habitat recording and a better awareness of the richness — and scarcity — of our surviving grasslands should encourage further conservation of this superb element of our natural heritage in Dorset.

ANIMALS OF GRASSLAND

This account has inevitably concentrated on the flora of grasslands, since this is the core of the habitat on which all associated animals depend. Some of these are relatively conspicuous or well-known, like grasshoppers and butterflies. Others, especially various insect and other invertebrate groups may be more numerous but less obvious, even though their part in the complex grassland ecosystem is just as vital. Spiders, plant-feeding bugs, snails, beetles and moths are among the many less visible fauna, though a few may be familiar. Greater and lesser bloody-nosed beetles and other smaller but more brilliantly coloured leaf beetles are more easily recognised, while several of the day-flying moths may also be easy to name.

GRASSHOPPERS AND CRICKETS

Many invertebrates are associated with grassland, but no other group combines the typical and familiar as effectively as the grasshoppers and crickets. Some are specialists of other habitats, like heath or mire, but a majority are encountered in some form of grassland.

The three common species, common green, meadow and common field may be found in many grasslands, including gardens as well as more special sites. The common green is the first to be heard in early summer and, like the meadow grasshopper, is perhaps most at home in lusher grass. The drier grasslands are favoured by the common field grasshopper, whose typical buff and fawn colours match the dried grass leaves of high summer. There are more spectacular colour forms to look out for though, including a stunning pink variant!

Another grasshopper frequently seen in certain grasslands, though traditionally characteristic of heathland, is the small mottled grasshopper. It is more strongly patterned than normal forms of the three common species and has either green or brown as its main colour. A particularly attractive green and grey form is good camouflage for the mottled grasshopper on open stony grassland

A long-winged conehead bush cricket.

The wart-biter cricket is one of Dorset's rarest insects.

sites like the sparse, lichen-rich turf of some downland tops, as at Bindon Hill.

Well grazed, warm downland slopes are the favourite habitat of the neat stripe-winged grasshopper, which is locally frequent in suitable sites in Dorset. The woodland grasshopper is even more localised, restricting itself to the longer grass of the woodland edge and other transitional sites. Where the lusher river valleys merge into saltmarsh is where to find the larger, evenly coloured lesser marsh grasshopper.

Though difficult to see and even harder to hear, two slender bush crickets — the long-winged and short-winged coneheads — are not uncommon, though nationally they are quite scarce. Until 1983 the long-winged conehead was very rare, but its rapid expansion from a few coastal flush sites into heathland in Dorset was noted at the same time as a similar increase in the New Forest. It has now spread right across southern England, occurring in longish grass in grassland as well as heathland sites, while the short-winged conehead prefers damper grassland with rushes. In contrast the decidedly chunky wart-biter cricket lives at only one site in Dorset. It is one of our rarest insects and is found otherwise only in Sussex and Wiltshire on single chalk downland sites with a mix of long and short flowery turf. The single Dorset population is on a mosaic of heath and acid grassland which provides shelter in the dwarf shrubs and food from the herb-rich patches of turf, a habitat maintained by grazing in one of the National Nature Reserves. Perhaps rarest of all, as well as the largest of the group is the mole cricket.

This well-named insect burrows in moist sandy soils and in the past was recorded from a few river valley sites. An individual was discovered in 1988 in a small paddock at Wareham. Despite its robust size and distinctive song, the mole cricket is a secretive insect and other populations may yet persist. Both it and the wartbiter should benefit from English Nature's Species Recovery Programme, which may yet snatch them from the brink of extinction and allow them to consolidate their tenuous hold in Dorset.

BUTTERFLIES AND MOTHS

An early summer walk on downland, like that at Hogcliff National Nature Reserve, should be rewarded by a sight of the six-spot burnet, burnet companion and wood tiger moths, flying among the butterflies and, if you are very lucky, the far less common cistus forester. The butterflies may well be represented by well over half of those known in the county. Longer grass will have clouds of meadow browns and marbled whites, with the commoner skippers. Hogcliff is one of the few chalk sites where marsh fritillary can be spotted on the abundant devil's-bit. On the opposite slope, in full sun and shorter turf, there will be adonis blue, grizzled skipper and later chalkhill, small blue and grayling. The local habitat variety provided on some sites by patches of scrub, with longer turf around and with sheltered alcoves, provides the niche for several species and reflects the subtleties in site conditions needed by different butterflies. So, in longer turf where the cowslips grow big, duke of burgundy may be

ABOVE *Marbled white butterflies mating.*
BELOW *A silver-spotted skipper butterfly.*

found and holly blue and green hairstreak will be happy. On short, open turf on hot slopes, but alas on few Dorset sites, silver-spotted skipper may be seen. In complete contrast, the rank tor grass turf of ungrazed sections of the coastal chalk and limestone is the home of the Lulworth skipper. Given its local abundance it is easy to forget that in England it is only found on Dorset's coastal grasslands.

BIRDS

Few of our birds are grassland specialists and, almost without exception, these are in decline. In wet grassland lapwing, snipe and redshank, once familiar in damp pastures, are now scarce nesting birds in Dorset, and the yellow wagtail, always more restricted, is confined to only one or two localities. Drainage and more intensive farming, which limits feeding, are the cause of the decline, which are countrywide. Even skylark and meadow pipit are less common, and though wheatears pass through on migration, their nesting in disused rabbit burrows in open turf may have all but ceased. A visitor to grassland and heath, from its woodland nesting habitat, is the striking green woodpecker. The principal attraction is insects to feed on, in particular an opportunity to raid the anthills so typical of our ancient downs and pastures.

Wet grassland in winter still attracts significant numbers of birds to some sites, so the Avon valley holds large flocks of wigeon and the smaller but nationally significant Bewick swan herd: the lower Frome also holds similar but smaller numbers. Occasional late floods can attract spectacular flocks of waders and wildfowl, like black-tailed godwits, and show the potential for such species, especially in sites close to their other feeding habitats like Poole Harbour.

Lapwings were once a common sight in damper pastures, but like all birds of wet grassland their numbers are declining.

MAMMALS

Many of our mammals are seen in grassland and it may form an important part of their range, though other habitats like woodland or hedgerows are also essential. Longer turf can often support large populations of voles and mice, and this in turn can provide one of the most appealing sites of grassland – though not for the voles! – a barn owl hunting at dusk. The activities of moles are obvious in grassland, and of importance in providing open patches and assisting drainage. The brown hare is too uncommon to have much effect, but rabbits are abundant and their impact is highly significant on many grassland sites. They are inevitably a mixed blessing. In some places they are the sole grazers, and wherever abundant modify the effect of other grazing and help limit the invasion of scrub.

A barn owl hunting at dusk.

FIVE

THE WOODLANDS

THE WOODLAND SCENE

Dorset, in common with the rest of lowland England, was almost entirely covered with natural broadleaved woodland after the last Ice Age. As the ice retreated northwards, 12-15,000 years ago, the tundra which lay in its wake became colonised by pioneer woodland followed by a more stable mixed woodland, with oak, ash, elm, lime and many other trees. This blanketing natural woodland, which covered everywhere except for open waters, high mountains and some cliffs, has become known as the 'wild-wood'. Think of it as a basic habitat which had to be cleared if the land it covered was to be used. As the human population increased, so more of the wild-wood was felled, initially mainly for agriculture, leaving just the small percentage that we see today.

With this in mind, it becomes fascinating to speculate which of our surviving woods are direct descendants of this original natural wild-wood. Has there been woodland on this site ever since the end of the Ice Age, or was it perhaps cleared in Roman times and then become wooded again? A wood that has a direct link to the natural woodland is known as primary woodland; old woodland on land that was cleared then re-wooded is known as ancient, and woods that have clearly re-colonised bare ground, or been planted, are known as secondary woods.

To ecologists, the age and origins of a wood are of great importance, not simply for historical reasons, but also because the oldest woods tend to

Autumn colour in woodland near Affpuddle.

have many more species – of all sorts – than more recent ones. From the nature conservation point of view, their complex soils, ancient coppice stools, and huge number of organisms, many of which we know little of, make them impossible to recreate. As we shall see later, there are plants that are almost exclusively confined to ancient woods.

However, virtually all woods, whether ancient or not, have been influenced by man over a long period, with centuries or even thousands of years, of coppicing and cutting, and they are described as semi-natural rather than wholly natural. They may have lost some of the species of the original woodland, through a gradual process of selection, but at the same time they have acquired others which have found the environment of a managed woodland to be congenial. Indeed many of the species which grow in Dorset's woods are adapted to traditional management regimes such as coppicing.

Today, less than 10% of Dorset lies under woodland, including plantations and other secondary woods. Important remaining blocks of woodland include Duncliffe, Piddles, Oakers, Chetterwood, Creech Great Wood, and those at Powerstock, Melbury, Edmonsham, Cranborne and on Cranborne Chase. There are many smaller, more isolated woods, which have ancient names – indicating a probable ancient origin – such as Holt, Buckshaw, Aldermore, Tincleton Hanging, Birches Copse and Heron Coppice. Most Dorset estates also have boundary woods and plantings, normally of more recent origin, with names such as Botany Wood, Jubilee Plantation or Zariba Clump. Then in addition to all these, there are conifer plantations, from small stands to extensive forests, many of them established in the last fifty years. The diversity of woodlands in the county provides wildlife habitats for many different plants and animals.

The word 'forest' may suggest great expanses of trees, but in Dorset the modern forests are plantations, managed by Forest Enterprise at Wareham, Puddletown, Moors Valley, Ferndown and elsewhere. The old forests were medieval institutions and royal hunting grounds, subject to forest laws. As well as woods and wood pasture, the forests were open areas of heath, downland, scrub, rough pastures and small settlements, and their woodland was a useful source of timber, firewood, venison, honey, birds for falconry, and revenue from law-breakers. Very little original woodland remains in the former Royal Forests of Dorset. Holt Forest is the last to survive as a place name on modern maps. Gillingham and Blackmore are now mostly farmland. Bere and Holt have new plantations and relic oaks. Purbeck, north of the hills, is heathland with large conifer plantations, and to the south is farmland with several small but ancient woods. Cranborne Chase is both extensive farmland and also long-established coppices and mixed plantings. Powerstock has a variety of plantations and regenerated woodland. Here and there a few small woods of great interest survive within the bounds of the old forests.

ANCIENT BROADLEAVED WOODLAND
Dorset's ancient woods and coppices are good wildlife habitats, and generally can be recognised by distinctive features. An ancient wood is usually small and isolated, and often adjoins a parish boundary beyond the meadows and arable fields of ancient settlements. Original wood boundaries are not straight, and their wood-banks are conspicuous, usually with a ditch on the outside. Any internal boundary banks are also irregular. The site is typically unsuitable for farmland, often on steep slopes or heavy, poorly-drained clay soil. The woods are deciduous apart from holly and many are hazel coppices, or coppice-with-standards dominated by oak or ash. Trees and other shrubs may have been coppiced. The soils are largely undisturbed and the top layers have a large and diverse population of invertebrates and many species of fungi, mosses and liverworts. Certain snails may indicate if the soil had ever been grassland. An ancient wood may also be identified by dense expanses of bluebells and other spring flowers. Some wild flowers associated only with ancient woods are wood anemone,

meadow saffron, woodruff, wood vetch, wood spurge, toothwort, herb paris, archangel, narrow-leaved lungwort, and several grasses and sedges. Bluebells have also survived for centuries in the open under bracken or on damp waysides where once there was woodland. Another indication is the remarkable variety of native trees and shrubs along the wood boundaries.

A very different approach to the search for ancient woodland involves using books, maps and documents in the archives of the Dorset County Records Office and elsewhere. Documentary evidence has proved invaluable when there is doubt about an ancient woodland site. Nine hundred-year-old Dorset Domesday records tell us which settlements at that time had woodland, and how much. Ancient woodland is unlikely to exist in places where none was recorded in 1086. Some woods are named in medieval documents and there can be no doubt of their antiquity: Broadley Wood near Bryanston, Marley Wood near Winfrith Newburgh, West Wood at Coombe Keynes, Bagman's Copse near Woodlands, Wilkswood north of Langton Matravers,

Wood anemones in Girdlers Coppice Nature Reserve, adjoining Piddles Wood.

Meadow saffron, which despite its name is one of the best indicators of ancient woodland.

Burwood at Cranborne, and any number of Colewoods where charcoal was once made.

There is also evidence of some ninety medieval deer parks where deer turned woodland into wood pasture, and many cases of woods where trees or underwood were stolen, or else destroyed by cattle. Woods in Blackmore, Cranborne Chase, Purbeck and Holt are shown on Tudor and early seventeenth century maps, and later, on maps made for some of the county estates. Of special interest is Isaac Taylor's 1765 one-inch map of Dorset, surveyed before treeplanting became widespread and the best single source of information about woodland in mid-eighteenth century Dorset. He shows over 200 identifiable woods, and all may be described as ancient woodland.

BELOW *Spring sunshine in Piddles Wood, one of the remaining oak woodlands in the county that dates back to the medieval period.*

Isaac Taylor's map of Dorset of 1765 is the best source of information about 18th century woodlands in the county, and although those in the list that follows have largely been replanted they all survive today.

West: Clifton, Honeycombe, Whitfield, Sleech, Hooke, Ridge, Powerstock, Batcombe, Middlemarsh, Armswell, Yellowham, Greys, Ilsington, Athelhampton.

North: Duncliffe, Brickles, Piddles, Holcombe, Humber (Mappowder), Turnworth, Houghton, Delcombe, Broadley, Ashley, Great Coll, Cranborne Chase (with Tarrant Gunville, Ashmore and Farnham).

South: Bere, Lychett, Charborough, East Lulworth, Winfrith Newburgh, Coombe Keynes, Creech, Brenscombe.

East: Harley Wood, Burwood, Boulsbury, Edmondsham, Birches Copse, Queen's Wood, Hinton Martell.

A drift of bluebells below coppiced oak and hazel in Milborne Wood.

COPPICES, PAST AND PRESENT

Since earliest times woods have been managed so as to produce a continuous supply of timber and underwood. Timber trees were close-grown to promote development of tall, unbranched trunks to be felled at maturity. However, if trees were cut or coppiced when young, new shoots could be selected to grow into long and slender poles. Poles were easily handled and had dozens of uses in rural communities. Multi-stemmed trees are still a familiar sight in Dorset woods: oak, ash, alder, sweet chestnut, sycamore, and even small-leaved lime near Cranborne and in King's Wood, Purbeck. One of the ancient coppiced oaks in the Milborne Woods has a 19ft. girth and supports ten massive poles up to 2ft. across. Most coppiced oaks are small because they were constantly lopped to produce a renewable supply for firewood and charcoal-making, and bark for tanning.

Hazel is commonplace in nearly every wood in the county and for centuries has been coppiced to yield rods and wands suitable for making thatching spars, hurdles and other rural products. Where hazel is shaded, overgrown and uncut, it eventually fails to regenerate. The practice of coppicing has declined since the last century except in a few scattered woods, notably in Cranborne, Cranborne Chase and between Dorchester and Blandford. Now it is being revived in other woods. Over-grown hazel is being cut for firewood or charcoal-making. New growth from cut stools is usually coppiced on a seven or eight year cycle, so that there are different stages of development within one wood as well as more light and space.

Pollarded trees, especially ash, were formerly cut about ten foot above ground to protect the re-growth from browsing cattle and deer, and old pollards are not uncommon on the boundaries of woods. Pollarded oaks of great age are a feature of ancient wood pasture, and can be seen in Holt Forest, The Oaks at Badbury Rings and in Melbury Park.

Coppice-with-standards woodland can be managed in ways which benefit wildlife, yet still produce a profitable crop. Timber has to be extracted with minimal disturbance to other vegetation; old trees, fallen branches and stumps are left to rot; open areas are created; unwanted brash from coppicing is used to protect hazel stools or make dead hedges; unnecessary bonfires and tidying up are avoided; rides and paths are maintained, and some areas of woodland are left undisturbed. In contrast, unmanaged and neglected woods become increasingly shaded and lose the diversity of habitats essential for many woodland plants and animals.

MIXED WOODS

Many woods are a mixture of broad-leaved trees and conifers, and include both introduced and native species. If these woods were planted or became established on old pasture or arable land they have no resemblance to ancient woodland. Some have been planted on sites of former woodland and still have hazel with bluebells, sedges and woodrush and other woodland flowers.

Beech trees are common in Dorset woods, and a familiar sight around parkland and estates, along boundaries and as avenues near Kingston Lacy

Hazel coppice ready for cutting in Garston Wood near Sixpenny Handley.

and on Cranborne Chase. Many have originated from plantings beginning in the second half of the eighteenth century. Few shrubs and flowers can grow in the heavy shade cast by beech apart from a few rare orchids and fungi. The tree does not appear to be a native in Dorset and has been widely introduced as a timber tree in modern plantations such as the Gardiner Woods above Springhead, and is often grown with conifers which help the saplings become established.

Beech in mixed woods may be associated with other introductions: sycamore, sweet chestnut, horse chestnut, Turkey oak, common lime, and poplars in damp spots. Holm oak is a useful evergreen. Mature hornbeam is rare. Conifers include European and Japanese larch, Scots and other pines, red cedar, Norway spruce, Douglas fir, and Western hemlock. They are generally grown for timber in blocks but single trees are common in estate woodland, often with Wellingtonia and coast redwood.

When some of the older estate woods were established to provide cover for game birds, alien shrubs such as snowberry, *Lonicera nitida*, laurel, box, and the invasive *Rhododendron ponticum* were introduced. Now many estate woods are overgrown and heavily shaded. Where there is ground flora, the difference from ancient woodland is obvious because the flowers of ancient woods are absent. In their place are nettles, ivy, hogweed, goosegrass, rough meadow-grass, herb robert, Yorkshire-fog, brambles and elder bushes. Sometimes a wood has signs of settlement or ridge-and-furrow from former farmland. Most estate woods have walls or fences and lack the conspicuous hedgebank-and-ditch of ancient woods.

The wildlife of mixed woodland is generally less plentiful and varied than in ancient woodland, but there are commonly habitats for pheasant, deer, grey squirrels and probably most of the woodland mammals. Bird life depends on available shelter and sources of food. Insects and other invertebrates occupy suitable places. Fungi appear in the autumn and the commoner lichens slowly become established on tree trunks.

Hoar frost on a line of beech trees near Beaminster.

TYPES OF TREES

NATIVE TREES AND SHRUBS

The earliest records we have of Dorset trees are from Stone Age and Iron Age charcoal found at Maiden Castle near Dorchester. There was oak, ash, willow, poplar, birch, elm, whitebeam and yew. The smaller trees were represented by hazel, crab, common buckthorn, hawthorn, service-tree, plum, cherry and blackthorn. From other records we can add lime, field maple and holly.

Pedunculate oak, its acorns on stalks, dominates much of Dorset's broad-leaved woodland. The sessile oak, more familiar in north and west Britain, is less abundant. Hybrids occur, also with the alien Turkey oak. The wildlife associated with woodland oaks is phenomenal because an oak tree can provide habitats for mammals, birds, moths, other invertebrates, insect galls, ferns, lichens, mosses, fungi, slugs and snails. Oak grows with holly and silver birch on more acidic soils, often with bracken or brambles. Silver birch rapidly colonises woodland clearings as well as damp heathland on sandy soils. Holly is heavily browsed by deer.

Ash grows alongside oak in many woods and is common on Dorset's chalk and limestone soils. Seedlings and saplings are plentiful but palatable and often eaten by deer. The ground flora is an expanse of dog's-mercury and ramsons, the pungent wild garlic. Old coppiced ash trees are a common feature of wood boundaries where branches, now massive, once were laid to form a hedge.

Field maple, which gives its name to Mapperton and Mappowder, grows with ash and hazel in many woods on the Dorset chalklands. It is also common in hedgerows; often with wayfaring-tree, common buckthorn, dogwood, spindle and hawthorn; sometimes with clematis and white bryony, and more rarely with whitebeam.

Sallow or grey willow is widespread in damp woods on poorly-drained soils. Where it has taken over old ponds and abandoned wetland, a sallow wood or 'carr' develops. Marsh violets flourish in some sallow woods on west Dorset greensands, and in wet places the poisonous hemlock water-dropwort is well-established. Both the silver and downy birch trees are common in sallow carrs. Such woods are generally secondary woodland and develop rapidly when land drainage has been neglected.

Alder is a tree along water courses and springs and forms small areas of woodland in wet places. The trees are often multi-stemmed, evidence of past coppicing when alder was valued for its wood and charcoal. It is long-established in ancient woodland, hence such names as Aldermore and Alderholt.

Wych elm has survived the effects of elm disease in ancient woods, notably at Badbury. But the widespread loss of the elm has caused the decline of that elusive butterfly, the white-letter hairstreak. English elm is regenerating as suckers in many hedgerows, even spreading into woodland, as at Wyke Wood near Abbotsbury.

Small-leaved lime and wild service-tree, both uncommon in Dorset, are found only on sites of ancient woodland. Small-leaved lime grows in a dozen places, mostly in the north and east of the county, and only in long-established estate woodlands. Lime trees were once regularly coppiced and the trees at Edmondsham and on the Hampshire border are centuries old. Archaeological evidence shows that lime trees were abundant in Britain until the Bronze Age, but they have became increasingly rare because young trees, growing from suckers and occasionally seed, are palatable and constantly at risk from grazing animals. Small-leaved lime as a woodland tree appears to have been displaced gradually by the more prolific oak tree.

Wild service-tree is now restricted to a few woods and former woodland boundaries in Piddles Wood and elsewhere in the north and west of the county. Seedlings are rare, probably because the fruits are eaten by small mammals and birds, but established trees produce numerous suckers which can become trees if not coppiced, chewed by deer, or too severely shaded.

Crab apple is a rather uncommon and solitary tree in ancient woods. It is a small tree, once valued for its hard wood and as rootstock for the scions or cuttings from other apple trees. Crab is distinguished by its dark and dense twiggy branches and small bitter fruits. Edible apples in woods are introductions near sites of habitation, often growing with elder bushes, nettles and other plants which need enriched soil.

Aspen is the only native poplar. It is locally frequent along the edges of damp woods on heavy soils, sometimes with the hybrid Grey poplars. Goat willow is a medium-sized woodland tree, and like sallow, an important food plant for caterpillars, and commonly occurs as a hybrid with other willows. Guelder rose may be found in the wetter woodland soils, and rowan, the mountain ash, in more acidic, sandy places. Gean or wild cherry was originally a native tree, but present trees are probably recent introductions.

Woodland hawthorn is almost unknown in Dorset but common hawthorn is in hedges everywhere, and on most wood boundaries where its fruits provide a bounty for birds in autumn. Blackthorn does not usually grow inside ancient woods, but soon invades clearings and spills out from wood edges on to pasture if not checked. Blackthorn scrub on old wooded commons or rough grassland is prominent at Powerstock, Lydlinch, Deadmoor and Povington, and is an ideal habitat for nightingales in spring and butterflies in summer.

Yew in Dorset woods appears to have been planted or introduced by birds; the only yew wood, on the south slopes of Hambledon Hill, is believed to be medieval in origin. Whitebeam, too, has been widely planted on calcareous soils but native trees are also widespread, and may be seen in Garston Wood and other parts of Cranborne Chase.

A conifer plantation at Powerstock Common.

PINE TREES AND OTHER CONIFERS

Scots pine was introduced into eighteenth century estate woodlands and the heathland of south-east Dorset where pine readily regenerates. Long-established pines on the islands of Poole Harbour and around Bournemouth are distinctive landscape features, contrasting sharply with the formal plantations on twentieth century estates where conifers of various kinds have been planted as timber trees. Notable conifer plantations, sometimes with lesser stands of broad-leaved woodland, are at Champernhayes, Chetterwood, Cranborne, Farnham, Duncliffe, Holt Forest, Hooke, Lulworth, Melbury, Middlemarsh, and Blandford. Other extensive plantations on former heathland are those of the Wareham Puddletown and Ferndown Forests, now managed by Forest Enterprise, and include plants of heath and heath bogs in open areas.

Plant and animal life is sparse among conifers compared to broadleaved woodland, and much poorer than in the countries from where the trees originated. Blocks of trees in a plantation are of one species, age and size and usually cast heavy shade. There may be birdlife and plenty of insects but vegetation tends to be restricted to mosses, ferns and fungi able to tolerate low levels of light. In several ways, conifers can influence the soil: their needles are slow to rot, leaf litter becomes increasingly acidic and buried seeds may not survive.

The picture changes when there are additional habitats in conifer plantations: grassy rides; damp spots with sallow, birch, rowan, holly and *Molinia*

The spotted longhorn beetle, a beetle adapted to living among conifers. The larvae feed in stumps and dead branches, and pupate in the woods in which they feed, often taking several years to mature.

grass; patches of bracken, bramble or heather; or old trees, stumps and fallen branches. Rides and clearings can be good places to find foxglove, fleabane and flowers of acidic grassland, also perhaps bilberry bushes or climbing corydalis, and, near Moreton, the rare heath lobelia. Areas where wood sorrel, wood spurge, woodrush and bluebells struggle to survive among the trees clearly indicate that the place was once ancient woodland.

Many insects are well adapted to living among conifers: longhorn beetles in stumps, bark beetles on pines, several pine-shoot moths and pine weevils in young shoots, numerous micro-moths and other moths on bark, including the pine hawk-moth, and the caterpillars of the bordered white moth on needles. The well-known wood-ant builds spectacular nests, constructed by thousands of worker ants from fallen needles, especially pine and spruce, and associated with the 7-spot ladybird. Three of Dorset's thirty-four ladybird species live on conifers, and two heathland butterflies, the grayling and silver-spotted blue occur in heathy places among pine trees. Flying insects are often preyed upon by bats, but bat boxes need to be provided because conifer trees are unsuitable for permanent bat roosts.

Dorset plantations have encouraged the rapid spread of sika and roe deer as the ranks of trees provide ideal cover when deer extend their territory. Bucks cause a lot of damage by fraying bark when they rub velvet from their antlers. Foxes, grey squirrels, and short-tailed voles are other common animals in many conifer plantations, and small populations of red squirrels survive among the mature pines of Brownsea and other Poole Harbour islands.

HEDGES AND THICKETS

Hedges are crucial to wildlife. They are like linear woodland, extending along roads and fields, and linking woods and copses which have become isolated in farmland. Best in Dorset are ancient hedgebanks, the former boundaries of Saxon parishes, medieval deer parks, estate woodland, old tracks and drove roads. In these long-established hedges you may find dogwood, buckthorn, wayfaring-tree, spindle, hazel, holly, as well as honeysuckle, clematis, black bryony, white bryony, briars and brambles. Sometimes there is butcher's-broom, not uncommon in north-east Dorset, but this unusual shrub may have been planted to fill gaps. Old trees in a hedge are likely to have been pollarded, coppiced or laid, and the number of different trees and shrubs is often found

An old holly hedge in the Dorset Wildlife Trust Nature Reserve at Kingcombe Meadows.

Bluebells, wild garlic, campion and yellow archangel in light shade at the foot of a Dorset hedge.

to correlate with the antiquity of a hedgebank.

The tangle of hedgebank vegetation provides many birds with excellent cover, nesting sites and a good supply of food. More than eighty kinds of moth caterpillars feed on hawthorn leaves alone. Hedgebanks are habitats where fox, badger and rabbit dig their holes. The deep, shady sides of hollow-ways, where a lane is lower than the fields each side, is ideal for ferns, mosses and liverworts. Less shady places may have primroses, violets and other woodland plants. A few hedges are the sites of Dorset rarities: wild tulip, small teasel and copse-bindweed.

Recent hedges have less diversity than old ones. Hedges along the rectangular fields of farmland were planted with elm, hawthorn or holly and other shrubs when the open landscape was enclosed during the eighteenth century and

later. Few mature elms have survived the devastating beetle-carried fungus responsible for Dutch Elm disease, but elm suckers are again a familiar feature. Newer hedges are lacking in woodland wild flowers but they are important sites for nesting and feeding birds, as well as corridors for bats and barn owls. When overgrown hedges are cut back by mechanical flailing and slashing, the shrubs eventually recover, but birds are forced to establish new territories. The revival of the art of hedge-laying in the Blackmore Vale, at Lower Kingcombe and other parts of Dorset has shown that a stockproof hedge may be a profitable alternative to a wire fence.

Most thorn thickets and scrub have been cleared from Dorset farmland; juniper is virtually extinct though thorn, gorse and brambles continue to invade ungrazed chalkland. Thorn and

A blackcap feeding its chicks. The blackcap is a summer visitor from the southern Mediterranean and Africa, arriving in April to breed. It nests in woodland thickets, well-grown with brambles or briars.

sallow thickets develop wherever there are abandoned pastures on soggy soils, including the unstable coastal undercliffs. All kinds of thickets are valuable bird habitats and left undisturbed become colonised by ash, maple and oak and eventually develop into natural woodland.

Other changing habitats are important. Of special interest are Dorset's young oak plantations on several estates, especially in the Blackmore Vale, as well as many roadside and other plantings of broad-leaved trees throughout the county. They are wildlife sites of the future and their natural history is unfolding.

WOODLAND WILDLIFE

FLOWERS AND FERNS

Woodland flowers are at their best in spring before the trees come into leaf and when there is more light and less competition from shrubs. Dorset's ancient coppiced woodland is especially rich in wild flowers. Many are found in the deep and slightly acidic loams of bluebell woods, some in drier chalk soils among dog's mercury and wild garlic and others in woodland of all kinds.

Some plants grow only in ancient woods and coppices and are not found in secondary woodland: Herb Paris, toothwort and yellow gagea; pale sedge and thin-spiked sedge; the three woodrushes, greater, hairy and southern woodrush; and the grasses, wood melick and wood millet. Ferns in woodland include hard fern, hard shield fern, scaly male fern and polypody, but most ferns can also grow in damp, shady hedgebanks where there are other familiar woodland flowers: primrose, violets, goldilocks and Dorset's 'spring messenger', the lesser celandine. Other plants, normally confined to ancient woodland and unable to spread to new places are: wood anemone, yellow archangel, bitter-vetch, wood vetch, wood spurge and the rare narrow-leaved lungwort of south-east Dorset. Wood anemone has proved to be an especially reliable indication of a site of ancient woodland wherever it grows.

Several familiar plants grow in both old woods and old pastures: wild daffodil, locally common on heavy soils in a narrow band across the county from the Devon border east to Edmondsham; meadow saffron, restricted to a few places such as Horse Close Wood in central Dorset; and pignut and betony, widespread on more acidic soils. Plants of old pastures such as lady's-mantle,

Early purple orchids, primroses and dog-violets growing in coppiced woodland at Woodbury Hill, Bere Regis.

The rare narrow-leaved lungwort in woodland at Doddings, Bere Regis.

long-stalked crane's-bill and adder's-tongue fern are to be found in the grassy rides of several ancient woods. Rides are also places where butterflies may feed on plants such as bugle, wild strawberry and common fleabane.

Woodland orchids grow in the humus-rich soils of both ancient woods and more recent plantations, notably beech. The helleborines seem to favour wood margins, especially on chalkland soils. Others, including bird's-nest orchid, tolerate deep shade, and some, including early-purple, butterfly and fly orchids, also grow in grassland. Orchid capsules full of minute seeds may be seen on old flower spikes at the end of the summer, but deer are a serious threat in some Dorset woods because they nip off the flowering spikes before the capsules can form. It is probable that insect pollinators are present in woodland, although self pollination is common in white helleborine and other orchids.

Wet places in woods are habitats for other plants. Damp spots often have clumps of wild red currant, possibly spread by birds; small streams are commonly lined with golden-saxifrage, including the rarer opposite-leaved golden-saxifrage in west Dorset; in a few wet woods there is water avens and its woodland hybrid. As well as ferns, sedges are usually plentiful, and more rarely, wood club-rush and wood horsetail, also in the west of the county.

Only a few plants can tolerate heavy shade in summer and the two saprophytes, yellow bird's-nest and bird's-nest orchid, are rare and hard to find. Other summer flowers are commoner in clearings and glades: hairy St John's-wort, orpine in Piddles Wood and a few other places, nettle-leaved bellflower on the Purbeck Hills and other chalk slopes, yellow pimpernel on clay, common cow-wheat and golden-rod on more acidic soils.

Some of Dorset's rarest plants are found in a single or else only a handful of places. Spring snowflake grows in a stream-side coppice in west Dorset, solomon's-seal in a wood in Cranborne Chase, and plants once used for medicine or poison, monkshood, mezereon, green hellebore and

Yellow bird's-nest, a rare plant of well-shaded beech woods.

stinking hellebore, occur in places which suggest that long ago they may have been introduced. Certainly, lily-of-the-valley and snowdrops in Dorset woods are recent introductions, but columbine was probably a wild plant before being brought into cottage gardens. Whatever their origin, these attractive plants add to the variety of Dorset's woodland flowers.

SMALL PLANTS

All woods have a selection of lichens, mosses and liverworts, familiar groups of plants not always easy to identify. Only a few have common names. Many are epiphytes, and grow on tree trunks and branches. Others grow on the ground, especially at the base of trees. They depend on the damp atmosphere and moist soil typical of woodland.

Dorset has good places for lichens; many of the 500 British lichens of shrubs and trees can be found in the county, except those formerly associated with mature elm trees, now dead. There are suitable sites in parks and damp, open woodlands where conditions are favourable: sufficient light, air relatively free of sulphur and other pollutants, little disturbance and a continuity of old trees. Oakers Wood near Bovington has an exceptional number of different kinds of lichens. Recent studies of these small plants have been encouraged by their role as indicators of clean air. They do not harm trees and may hide insects and provide useful nest material for long-tailed tits and other songbirds.

The main groups of bark lichens – leprose, crustose, foliose, and fruticose – are well represented. The nature of the bark is important, its texture, acidity and position on the tree. Many kinds of lichen can be found on hazel and holly, and on the rougher bark of ash, maple and oak. The venerable oak trees in the wood pasture of Melbury deer park are renowned for many rare species, including *Lobaria amplissima*, one of the four lungwort lichens.

Mosses often share a 'mini-habitat' with lichens, liverworts and even green algae. They grow tightly in tufts, clumps, patches or cushions wherever conditions are suitable for them to get established. Mosses such as *Dicranum majus*, *Frullania tamarisci*, *Plagiothecium undulatum*, and *Rhytidiadelphus loreus* are found in ancient woodland. Wet and shady woods are ideal for *Plagiorinum undulatum* and *Thamnobryum alopecurum*, and liverworts such as *Lophocolea cuspidata* and *Plagiochila asplenioides*. Common woodland mosses include species of *Atrichum*, *Eurhynchium*, *Hypnum*, *Mnium*, *Orthotrichum*, *Ulota*, pale cushions of *Leucobryum glaucum* and the beautiful, fern-like *Thuidium tamariscum*.

WOODLAND FUNGI

Fungi in woods are mostly unseen, their fungal threads or hyphae feeding on leaf litter, twigs, droppings and fallen branches, helping to create humus and enriching the soil with nutrients. They are an indispensible part of the cycle of decay and renewal in woodland life, and promote tree growth when their hyphae are united as mycorrhiza with tree roots.

The appearance of larger fungi, better known as mushrooms or toadstools, is irregular and unpredictable. These fungal fruiting bodies are capable of producing astronomical numbers of reproductive spores. A toadstool may be restricted to one type of woodland: on poor, acid soils under conifers or birch, or richer soils under oak, or chalky soils under beech. Some grow only in unusual habitats: a pine cone, an oak leaf, a dead insect, a pile of dung, an old bonfire site. Most species occur countrywide and are not confined to any one county. Dorset woods provide good habitats and fungi are plentiful in ancient woodland: for example, Bracketts Coppice in north Dorset has over 400 species.

Conspicuous fungi have been given English names: parasites such as dryad's saddle, on ash

Porcelain fungus, one of over 400 species of fungi to have been counted in Bracketts Coppice, near Corscombe, a Dorset Wildlife Trust Nature Reserve.

and several other trees, slimy beech caps on old beech trees, beefsteak fungus on oak, honey fungus on many trees; saprophytes such as sulphurtuft and orange pholiota on stumps; stinkhorn under conifers; milkcaps and bright-coloured russulas under mature trees; brain fungus and witches butter on branches. A special group are the symbiotic fungi in lichens on bark and stumps.

Edible fungi are also well-represented in Dorset woods and include wood mushroom, wood blewitt, cep or penny bun, and hedgehog fungus in mixed woods; chanterelle, usually under oak; horn-of-plenty in deep moss; oyster mushroom on fallen branches; cauliflower fungus at the base of mature conifers; and in most woods, more russulas and milkcaps. A wood with clearings or grassy rides may have other edible species: parasols, shaggy inkcap, even giant puffball.

Fungi poisonous to man are widespread: the deadly death-cap and other *Amanita* in many woods, fly agaric under birch, and several brown-spored species of *Hebeloma, Entoloma, Conocybe*

and *Inocybe* – all of which are best left untasted. Yet mushrooms and toadstools are regularly eaten by deer, badgers, squirrels, voles, woodmice, snails, slugs and the larvae of numerous beetles, flies, gnats and micro-moths. Fungi may be an important source of food for many creatures before winter sets in, and there is a strong case against over-collecting in autumn.

INSECTS AND THEIR RELATIVES

Insects live in all kinds of Dorset woodland and make use of every available habitat. Over 200 different insects have been found on oak trees alone and in ancient woods there may be several thousand, some uncommon and others familiar, in both larval and adult form.

Ground beetles and springtails are plentiful in soil and leaf litter, and flies and dung beetles wherever there are animal droppings. Other beetles include cardinal beetles, stag beetles and longhorns which occupy rotten tree-stumps, together with earwigs, sawflies and hover-flies. Other creatures

BELOW *The poisonous fly agaric toadstool.*

OPPOSITE PAGE *A silver-washed fritillary butterfly.*

at ground level are centipedes, millipedes and woodlice, slugs on fungi and succulent plants, spiders, mites and ticks, including the disease-carrying deer tick. Earthworms occur in soil which is neither too wet nor too acidic. Snails of several kinds are plentiful in lime-rich woodland soils and may be preyed upon by glow-worm larvae.

Large numbers of insects live on tree trunks, including the ash bark beetle and the notorious elm bark beetle, responsible for spreading the fungus which destroys elm trees. Other examples from Dorset woods are the larvae of moths such as the red-necked footman which feed on lichens, and robber flies, snake flies and bark bugs which feed upon insect larvae. Many moths and micromoths are concealed on bark by their cryptic colouring. Bumble bees, hornets and tree wasps make nests in tree holes, and honey bees colonise convenient hollows.

The leaves of most woodland trees are liable to attack from insect larvae, especially in spring. The green oak tortrix caterpillars can defoliate oak trees, and both buff-tip and winter moth caterpillars damage various broad-leaved trees. Other leaf insects include species of bugs, weevils and other beetles, as well as leaf miners.

Large numbers of insects and other invertebrates are eaten by birds and small mammals. Whilst shrews and hedgehogs are concealed among leaf litter and fallen branches, birds are active at all levels in well-structured woodland. Crane-flies, gnats and mosquitoes are taken by flycatchers, whilst once night has fallen other flying insects, including cockchafers and dung beetles, are eaten by woodland bats.

Thirty-eight of Dorset's butterflies breed in woods. Each has special requirements and depends on woodland structure, wood margins and the land beyond. Other essentials are oak or other trees, shrubs, brambles and climbers, a continuity of coppicing, sunny glades, flowers in spring, winding paths, open grassy rides and damp, flower-filled ditches. Woodlands in such places as Cranborne Chase, Deadmoor, Powerstock and Bracketts Coppice are rich butterfly sites because they provide many of these features.

The purple emperor is rarely seen in Dorset. Even more elusive is the white-letter hairstreak, which requires mature elm. In the larger oakwoods there are colonies of both purple hairstreak and white admiral, and, depending on coppicing and the availability of common dog-violet, the fritillary butterflies, pearl-bordered, small pearl-bordered and silver-washed. The high brown fritillary is apparently restricted to a single Dorset wood.

Some butterflies such as hedge and meadow browns, marbled and other whites, dingy and grizzled skippers, are common in woodland glades and grassy rides. In shadier places and among shrubs are holly blue, speckled wood, green hairstreak and brimstone, the latter attracted to common buckthorn on chalkland and purging buckthorn on acidic heathland soils. Many colonies of woodland butterflies disappeared during years when hazel coppices were abandoned and became overgrown and shady. With the renewal of coppicing in both private woods and nature reserves, butterflies have a better chance of survival, and the re-introduction of a few species, notably the wood white in west Dorset has proved a success.

REPTILES

Different habitats in woodland may be occupied by other animals such as reptiles. Woodland clearings, especially when stumps and branches have been left, are warmer and lighter than in surrounding woodland and suitable for adders and grass snakes. Toads are not uncommon, and there are likely to be frogs and newts feeding on aquatic insects in ponds. All the British snakes and lizards of heathland may also inhabit sandy clearings in mature pine plantations.

The rare wood white butterfly survives in one or two woodland sites in the county.

BIRDS

Birds of woodland in lowland Britain are well represented in Dorset. Garston Wood in Cranborne Chase is a good example of old woodland where birds are plentiful. Here there are trees and shrubs of all ages and a wide range of habitats: perches, song posts, tree stumps, nesting sites and a supply of food. The ground layer of the wood provides a constant food supply: small plants, mosses, seeds, acorns, insects, spiders worms, snails, as well as leaf litter and dead branches to hide in. Then the 'field' layer with its ferns, flowering plants, low bushes and brambles, ideal for scrub warblers and other small birds. The higher undergrowth of thorn trees, coppiced hazel or other shrubs provides nesting sites for thrushes and blackbirds. Above, in the tree canopy, willow warbler, wood warbler and chiffchaff feed among the leaves, and on branches near the tree-tops, woodpigeons, crows, buzzards and sparrowhawks can make their nests.

Holes and hollows in standing trees are ideal nesting sites for the nuthatch, tree creeper, great spotted woodpecker and tawny owl. Glades and

On this and the following page are just some of the remarkable variety of birds that can be found in Dorset's woods.

TOP   *A sparrowhawk on the nest.*

ABOVE   *A buzzard.*

RIGHT   *A tawny owl.*

RIGHT *A great spotted woodpecker.*

BELOW *A treecreeper returning to its nest with a spider.*

BOTTOM *A song thrush feeding its young.*

more open areas are hunting-grounds for the spotted flycatcher. Young hazel coppice is suitable for nesting garden warblers. Thickets inside the wood attract nightingales in spring, and brambles provide winter shelter for redwing, fieldfare, redpoll, even brambling, as well as resident birds. Woodland territories are established by most of the familiar birds of gardens and hedges: robin, blackbird, wren, dunnock, song thrush, mistle thrush, bullfinch, greenfinch, and all the common tits.

A few birds are attracted to pine plantations in search of insects and nest sites. The green woodpecker digs into wood ant nests, and the great spotted woodpecker feeds on bark insects and conifer seeds. Goldfinch, chaffinch and various tits are often among younger trees, and siskin and goldcrest are not uncommon in tree-tops. Jays, magpies and wood pigeons are generally frequent and dead trees are important perches for birds of prey, including the hobby. Birch trees and sallow on the edge of plantations are additional habitats for tits and summer warblers. In winter, the crossbill occasionally arrives from the north to feed on the seeds of pine cones.

Some estate woodland, originally planted with beech, chestnut or sycamore, often has a dense undergrowth of rhododendron and other alien shrubs with little birdlife. Where pheasants are reared, finches and other seed-eaters take advantage of their food, whilst damp, grassy rides may attract woodcock. However, Dorset's planted woods lack the diversity of habitats found in long established broad-leaved woodland.

DEER

Deer have a profound effect on woodland. They damage trees by fraying the bark, prevent natural regeneration by eating tree seedlings and saplings, and retard the regrowth of coppiced hazel. Where young trees are protected by tree-guards and fencing, unprotected areas become more vulnerable. Large herds of deer eventually destroy undergrowth and turn well-structured woodland into wood pasture, or 'high forest', with only

A young roe deer. Roe are now widespread wherever there is woodland, even invading gardens, and their numbers are on the increase.

mature trees. Our woods are home to roe, fallow, sika and muntjac deer. The few red deer are rarely seen, and are the descendants of those that once escaped from parks. Muntjac, a recent arrival in Dorset, is small and secretive, but is becoming more widespread than occasional reports suggest. Sika were introduced to Brownsea Island in the last century and escaped to the mainland. Herds of sika are not uncommon in and around the conifer plantations of the heathlands of south-east Dorset and are extending their range.

Fallow deer are long-established in the county. In medieval times they were protected for the chase and also kept in deer parks, surrounded by high banks and stout palings. Medieval woodland was managed for the benefit of 'the venison and the vert', to the detriment of trees that were browsed by deer, especially in winter when food was scarce. Fallow deer are still kept in a few parks, notably Stock Gaylard, but most now browse in well-wooded places such as Powerstock and Cranborne Chase, where they do considerable damage in hazel coppices as well as on the surrounding farmland.

Roe deer are widespread wherever there is woodland. In ones or twos they emerge to feed at dawn and dusk, ranging over farmland, hedges and gardens before hiding in dense thickets during the day. They are bigger than the roe of eastern England and their numbers are on the increase. Unlike other deer they fray tree-bark in spring, when trees are most vulnerable. They feed on a wide range of plants, including grasses and herbs, tree shoots, leaves and berries. In winter, deer activity can be assessed by the degree of browsing on holly shoots before the new shoots of coppiced hazel and ash are attacked in spring.

BATS

Fourteen species of bats occur in Britain and all have been recorded in Dorset. They are nocturnal and may be seen flying at dawn and dusk when they feed almost exclusively on insects. Many places are important for their food supply, ponds, marshy meadows, old pastures, hedges and trees. Although their natural roosts are woods and caves, most bats also use buildings for their summer roosts, and underground crevices in which to hibernate.

They also make use of hollows in trees and stumps, thickets and scrub, old hedgebanks with tall pollards, and continuous hedges linking summer roosts to feeding areas. Insects are plentiful in conifer plantations but natural roosting places are lacking. The long-eared bat is not uncommon in mature woodland. Only the serotine and greater and lesser horseshoe bats do not use hollow trees, but like other species they take advantage of woodland borders for spring feeding.

The two very rare species, Bechstein's and Leisler's, may depend wholly on mature woodland. The noctule, barbastelle, pipistrelle, Daubenton's, whiskered and probably Brandt's bats may choose either trees or buildings for their summer roosts and trees for hibernation.

A young stoat.

OTHER MAMMALS

Many animals spend at least part of their time in woodland, even water vole, otter and mink where river banks are adjacent. Hedgehogs inhabit open woodland as well as hedges. Both the common shrew and pygmy shrew live in woods where there are hollows, stumps, grasses and rushes, and plenty of insects to eat. The bank vole and short-tailed or field vole can also survive in grassy parts of woods, particularly where tree guards provide 'safe houses' in young plantations. They eat almost anything and in turn are food for larger animals and birds of prey. Two closely-related mice, the elusive yellow-necked field mouse and the long-tailed field mouse inhabit woods, and the latter, confusedly called a wood mouse, is also common in gardens and hedgebanks. All these small animals may be active both day and night throughout the year. Only the hedgehog and dormouse are true hibernators.

The smaller mammals tend to be shy and retiring, Though use is made of reports from naturalists, it is difficult to be certain of their numbers and spread. Other records depend on live trapping-and-release, or from casualties of cats or bits of bone in owl pellets. There may also be indirect signs such as teeth-marks on nuts, tracks in mud or a small stockpile of flowerbuds. The dormouse, protected and rarely seen, attracts more widespread interest. It is known to live in several Dorset woods where coppiced hazel is dense enough for its arboreal habits and also produces plenty of nuts. The haws of hawthorn provide an alternative food and strands of old honeysuckle may be used in their nests, together with moss, twigs, leaves and grass. Summer nests are high up in the bushes, and winter nests are among brambles or on the ground, in and under cut hazel stools. Dormice also make their nests in nest boxes designed for birds.

Signs of other animals are common: badger setts, rabbit burrows, fox earths, mole hills, even the 'form' of hares, a reminder that woods give shelter in an insecure countryside, particularly in winter. Foxes, weasels and stoats are well-known predators but polecats and pine martens became extinct in Dorset by the middle of the last century. Grey squirrels, the well-established 'tree rats' from North America, are widespread and numerous. They destroy birds' eggs and cause extensive damage to most trees, attacking bark, fruits and shoots. They have displaced red squirrels in woodland throughout England. In Dorset, red squirrels survive in small numbers among the pine trees of three Poole Harbour islands, including Brownsea. Great efforts are being made to save the red squirrel and dormouse from extinction in Dorset by preserving their habitats.

A hedgehog picking its way through fallen oak and beech leaves.

SIX

RIVERS AND STREAMS

THE VARIETY OF RIVERS

To the naturalist, a stream or river adds a special element to the landscape and the opportunity to enjoy a wide variety of plants and animals. Even an unhurried look from a bridge or a leisurely walk along a river bank can start to work its magic. How can plants, invertebrates and fish survive in this watery environment which is literally flowing past them to the sea? A brief glimpse of a trout taking an emerging mayfly or a dragonfly patrolling its bankside territory reminds us that this complex ecosystem links water, land and air.

From source to mouth, the only certainty about a river is that it flows one way, gathering tributaries as it drains a progressively larger area. Throughout this journey the temperature and flow regime, the slope and substratum, and many other features, show progressive change downstream, allowing the development of a sequence of habitat types, each with its own characteristic plants and animals.

The management of our rivers to balance the varied demands we place on them is a complex task, involving the active collaboration of many different organisations. The newly-formed Environment Agency (EA) has the leading role in this process, with duties which include the conservation and enhancement of wildlife in rivers. English Nature has more detailed statutory duties

The River Stour at Fiddleford Mill near Sturminster Newton.

for the promotion of nature conservation, and works in close cooperation with the EA to maintain and enhance the biological diversity and natural features of our rivers. Since 1963, scientists at the River Laboratory of the Institute of Freshwater Ecology (IFE) near Wareham have studied the chemistry and biology of rivers in Dorset and further afield. As a result, many of the rivers in the county have been studied in detail, enhancing our knowledge of this valuable resource.

The basic features of a river system are determined by the local geology, climate and topography, and further influenced by man's use of the catchment. The variety of geological formations in Dorset, from the older Jurassic rocks in the north and west, through the central outcrop of Cretaceous chalk to the younger Tertiary deposits of the Poole Basin in the east, are responsible for the variety of its rivers. The climate is mid-temperate with a maritime influence and the modest rainfall of around 900mm, together with the rounded topography of the chalk, ensures that most of the rivers are essentially lowland in character.

The drainage pattern for the three major Dorset river systems is south-easterly. The rivers Frome and Piddle, both fine examples of chalk streams, pour into Poole Harbour, whilst the River Stour, which drains more complex geology, flows into Christchurch Harbour.

For naturalists and fishermen alike, the mention of a chalk stream conjures up a vision of crystal-clear water where trout lie motionless between beds of swirling green weed. To understand why these streams give such a clear view of life below the water surface, we need to trace them to their source within the chalk itself. When rain falls on chalk downland, a high proportion moves directly through the soil and into the underlying chalk, instead of running directly off the land. Chalk is porous, but full of cracks and fissures, so the water moves downwards to accumulate as a huge underground reservoir known as an aquifer. In practice, it takes a long time for this groundwater to move down through the chalk and then laterally to emerge in the form of springs. As a result, chalk streams have several distinctive characteristics.

Firstly, they have a relatively stable flow regime. Winter rains normally replenish the aquifer to give peak flows in late winter and early spring, before the flow gradually decreases through the summer and autumn. Secondly, spring water normally emerges at about 11 degrees centigrade throughout the year, so chalk streams tend to be warm in winter, but cool in summer when compared to rivers which lack a major groundwater component. Thirdly, the slow filtration of the rainwater through the chalk and the limited surface run-off explain why chalk streams emerge so crystal-clear. In addition, the water itself is calcareous and rich in major plant nutrients. Finally, because the stream is dependant upon the water level within the chalk, the spring source is not a fixed location. Replenishment of the aquifer in winter allows the most upstream 'winterbourne' section to flow until falling water levels in the chalk cause it to dry up. The stream then flows from permanent springs at the perennial head, and life in the winterbourne must await the breaking of the springs next winter. The problems to be overcome when living in a winterbourne provide a stark contrast to the ideal conditions for plants and animals in the perennial section downstream!

Both the rivers Frome and Piddle are fed by a series of small chalk stream tributaries before crossing Tertiary beds in their middle and lower reaches. Here, their flow regimes have a higher component of surface run-off than classic chalk streams, resulting in a rapid rising of water levels and clouding of the water at times of high rainfall. For many centuries, our chalk streams have received active management by man, and their side channels, abandoned water meadow systems and associated wetlands add to their interest and importance.

The catchment of the River Stour is approximately twice the area of the Frome and Piddle combined, and although it extends into Somerset

The River Frome near Wool in spring, with a sallow in flower on the left bank and a mute swan in the background.

and Wiltshire, it is very much the Dorset Stour. Geologically the catchment can be divided into three main sections, the lower two being chalk and Tertiary beds, as in the Frome and Piddle. The upper section, which sets the character of the main river, includes a variety of Jurassic beds which give rise to soils with a high clay content. In consequence, this area, including the Blackmore Vale, has numerous tributaries which are prone to flooding due to the rapid surface run-off. Once the Lodden, Cale and Lydden have joined the Stour, the main river passes onto the wide belt of chalk where further tributaries are few, as is normal in chalk country. However, one notable chalk stream, the River Allen, joins the Stour at Wimborne, after which the river passes onto Tertiary deposits

before meandering its way to Christchurch Harbour. Before this final stage, one more tributary meets the Stour. The River Crane rises on chalk just north of Cranborne, but is renamed as the Moors River once it crosses Tertiary deposits. Despite its modest proportions, this river and its tributary, the Uddens Water, encompass both calcareous and acidic waters and support such a spectacular variety of plant and animal life that it has the status of a Site of Special Scientific Interest (SSSI).

Similar recognition has been afforded the River Avon, which though largely within Wiltshire and Hampshire, slips into Dorset as it nears its journey's end in Christchurch Harbour. Most recently, a section of the River Frome between Dorchester

LEFT *The slow-moving River Brit near Netherbury. The Brit rises in the hills above Beaminster, flowing to the sea at West Bay.*

OPPOSITE PAGE *Water crowfoot in flower on the River Frome at Frampton.*

and Wareham, representing the most westerly example of a major chalk stream has also been proposed for SSSI status.

There are, of course, many other streams and rivers in Dorset which help mould the landscape. The rivers Axe and Yeo rise in the north-west, only to leave the county, but in the south-west the rivers Char and Brit complete their short course to the coast. The complex geology of this corner of Dorset results in striking scenery and swift-flowing streams which flow through Charmouth and Bridport. A little further east, the River Bride flows in a westerly direction from near Hardy's Monument through more gentle countryside to the sea at Burton Bradstock. Continuing eastwards, several small streams pour into the Fleet and Weymouth Bay, most notably the River Wey itself, which ends its journey at Radipole Lake, an urban treat for birdwatchers.

Within Purbeck, the twin arms of the Corfe River flow through farmland on Wealden Clay resulting in a flashy river which then bursts through the Purbeck hills and over the Tertiary beds to Poole Harbour. Further north, within the Harbour, after the Frome and Piddle have released their waters into the Wareham Channel at Swineham Point, the Sherford River meets the same channel via Lytchett Bay. It rises from springs in the chalk near Bloxworth, but for most of its length it journeys through heavily wooded areas, including Wareham Forest and then farmlP

PLANTS

Even a short river-side walk in Dorset brings home the importance of plants in lowland rivers. The plant life in a mountain stream may be dominated by mosses and algae on rocks and boulders, but, in Dorset, many rivers have an abundance of higher plants adapted for life within, on the surface and at the margins of the river. Apart from their aesthetic appeal, plants have a major effect on the movement of water and sediments and create a variety of habitats which are used by invertebrates, fish, birds and mammals. We are all familiar with the role of plants in the food chain and the sight of a mute swan eating water crowfoot has much in common with cows cropping grass. But in truth, only a small proportion of fresh weed is normally consumed by the invertebrate or vertebrate fauna. In spring and summer, submerged plants offer a large surface area for the growth of algae, which are then grazed by invertebrates. In autumn, the weed starts to decay, but it also acts as a trap for autumn-shed leaves and together these food sources sustain many invertebrates through the winter.

Plant communities vary with river type. Along the length of a chalk stream, for example, species composition changes from source to mouth. In the winterbourne section, fool's watercress and common watercress may occur within and at the margins of the stream, whilst water crowfoot can show spectacular growth in spring, before assuming a different growth form as the stream dries out in summmer. Further downstream, where flow is permanent, water crowfoot continues to dominate, and its dark green beds produce an aerial patchwork of white-petalled flowers above the water surface in spring and early summer. Other

submergents include water-starwort, which forms elongated light green beds in slack silted areas, and lesser water-parsnip which grows as a creeping carpet of weed, favouring areas where bankside trees offer partial shade across the river.

A number of rivers in Dorset, including the Frome and Piddle, are important for a submergent weed with bright green finely divided leaves, river water-dropwort. This species is confined to north-western Europe and although it is relatively common in southern England, it deserves careful management because it is more common here than anywhere else in Europe.

Downstream, the variety of emergent and marginal plants increases. Reed sweet-grass, reed canary-grass and branched bur-reed provide refuge from mid-stream flows for a wide range of invertebrates below the water line and resting places for adult insects above water. In addition, greater willow herb, meadowsweet, comfrey, purple loosestrife and other flowers offer an ever-changing patchwork of colour along the river bank.

The less predictable flow regime of the River Stour and its tributaries presents problems for some plants in winter, but the lower flows in summer allow rich communities of submerged, floating and emergent plants to flourish. The clay substratum encourages the development of the common clubrush and the yellow water-lily, which produces thin leaves below the waterline plus thick floating leaves alongside its bright yellow flowers at the surface.

The Moors River below the Uddens confluence is a nationally recognised example of a small yet species-rich watercourse, but the Stour itself has its own treasures. Apart from its rich plant communities it also plays host to some rare aquatic plants. The Loddon pondweed (*Potamogeton nodosus*) is one such species, which grows in gravelly reaches between Child Okeford and Blandford on the Stour. The native sub-species of the summer snowflake (*Leucojum aestivum*) is also rare, but may be found between Blandford and Wimborne on the river bank and on islands within the river.

River water dropwort in flower on the River Stour.

INVERTEBRATES

Most naturalists soon become confident at identifying marginal aquatic plants, although some of the submerged species can be problematic! In contrast, the huge variety of invertebrates in running waters is sometimes discouraging to those with an interest in naming the major types. This is unfortunate, because some knowledge of the variety and adaptations of invertebrates, together with a basic understanding of their role in the ecosystem, brings its own reward.

In Dorset, many streams and rivers support a variety of non-insects, including flatworms (Tricladida), snails (Gastropoda), mussels (Bivalvia), true worms (Oligochaeta), leeches (Hirudinea) and crustaceans (Malacostraca), together with a somewhat wider range of insects. These may include representatives from most but not necessarily all of the major groups, including mayflies (Ephemeroptera), stoneflies (Plecoptera), dragonflies and damselflies (Odonata), bugs (Hemiptera), beetles (Coleoptera), alderflies (Megaloptera), caddis (Trichoptera) and true flies (Diptera).

The fauna at a particular site is largely determined by the environmental conditions, and therefore the type of river and the location of the site downstream are important in determining the invertebrate community. However, pollution and other forms of environmental stress can also affect the range of species, and the sensitivity of the invertebrate fauna to stress has been used in the biological monitoring of rivers for a number of years.

Many high quality sites in the middle reaches of our rivers include over a hundred species of invertebrates, with life cycles ranging from a few weeks to two years or more. One way through this confusing variety is to allocate species to 'functional feeding groups' in an attempt to understand their role in the scheme of things. For example, the freshwater shrimp, which occurs in high densities in the chalk streams is a 'shredder', performing an essential role in breaking down and consuming autumn-shed leaves. In this way it makes small particles available to other invertebrates and by converting coarse organic material into its own body tissue, it provides an important source of food for fish, including the bullhead and brown trout. Algae, which use both submerged leaves and gravel as a surface for attachment, are cropped by 'grazer-scrapers', including snails and caddis with a preference for hard surfaces, and some mayfly nymphs and non-biting midge larvae on plant surfaces.

The progressive breakdown of tree leaves, water weeds and algal material results in the production of fine particles within the water column and on the river bed. The so-called 'collector-filterers', notably blackfly larvae, passively filter the water for fine suspended material using their impressive head fans, whilst on the river bed the 'collector-gatherers', including the true worms (Oligochaeta), consume fine material in a further recycling process. In addition to these four main feeding groups there are, of course, invertebrate predators. Amongst the non-insects, individual species of flatworms and leeches have their own target prey organisms. In the insect predators, different feeding mechanisms and patterns of behaviour contribute to the success of the immature stages of dragonflies, alderflies, some

A golden-ringed dragonfly, a rare dragonfly usually found in water meadows.

A scarce chaser dragonfly, for whom Dorset's rivers provide a nationally important habitat.

need for awareness and sympathetic land management to ensure that these vulnerable streams are safeguarded is now a priority.

Within the middle and lower reaches of the Frome and Piddle, we find rich invertebrate communities with a wide variety of mayflies, caddis and true flies. The more gentle flow and the year-round availability of different habitats and food allow both rivers to support high densities of non-insects and insects. Whereas chalk streams have long been recognised for the richness and abundance of their communities, it is now apparent that parts of the Stour and some of its tributaries are also species-rich. A recent study of the Moors River and Uddens Water yielded 322 taxa, and regular monitoring by the Environment Agency is providing evidence that the lower Stour is also exceptionally rich.

A number of rarities occur at some of these sites, most notably the scarce chaser dragonfly (*Libellula fulva*), for whom Dorset is an important location. After emergence in late May, adults may be found in the lower Frome, Stour (including the Moors River) and the lower Avon. Some mention must also be made of the notorious 'Blandford Fly' (*Simulium posticatum*), which can inflict painful bites on people. Detective work and ingenuity by scientists from the IFE has revealed critical features in the life cycle of this blackfly, and the means to control it. This particular species has only one annual generation and in July the females, having previously taken a blood meal, deposit their eggs in the dry vertical banks of the River Stour. There they remain until late winter, when rising water levels wash them into the river. The larvae then hatch, attach to water plants and start to filter feed on the planktonic algae which are abundant in the river each spring. Once growth is complete, they pupate on the weed before emerging as adults in late May and June. After careful evaluation, this insect is now being controlled in an environmentally friendly manner, by spraying the larval habitat with a bacterium which is filtered from the water by the larvae. Once within the gut, a toxin is activated which is fatal to the larvae.

caddis and true flies. In this way, the invertebrates perform an essential role in the functioning of the river system by processing a wide range of food resources and making them available to the next trophic level, predominantly the fish.

The unique character of winterbournes and the problems faced by invertebrates attempting to colonize them are of particular interest within Dorset. A survey of the South Winterbourne stream in the early 1970s led to the discovery of a blackfly (*Metacnephia amphora*) new to science. The larvae grow during the early spring when the stream is flowing and complete their life cycle in two months, thus avoiding the drying of the stream in summer. Although this species has now been found at a small number of sites, including several winterbourne streams in the chalk belt of the Stour catchment, it remains rare. A similar strategy of spring growth and emergence is adopted by a species of mayfly, whose eggs remain in the dry stream bed until the return of flow the following winter.

More recent studies on a variety of headwater streams within the Stour catchment, and elsewhere in Dorset, have revealed that other rare and vulnerable species are characteristic of and frequently confined to headwater streams. The

Most aquatic insects leave the water to complete their life cycle, which is inevitably when they are most easily seen. In late April, a caddisfly, the Grannom, bursts from its pupal case on water crowfoot to emerge, feed and mate before laying a green mass of gelatinous eggs below the waterline, thus completing its annual cycle. In late May, the fisherman's mayfly (*Ephemera danica*) having spent two years as a nymph, feeding on small particles within its burrow, risks all as it rises to the water surface and attempts to fly off before being snapped up by vigilant trout. Mayflies are unusual in that 'subimagos' emerge from the water and a further skin must be cast to produce the full adult or 'imago'. The adults do not feed but, after mating, the larger females deposit several thousand eggs on the water surface. The eggs then sink to the bottom and stick to the substratum before hatching. Some species of mayflies fly upstream before depositing their eggs to counteract the tendency for the larval stages to drift downstream.

Each group of insects has its own particular strategy. Whereas the eggs of alderflies are deposited on marginal vegetation to enable the hatching larvae to fall into the water, many of the more familiar dragonflies and damselflies carefully deposit individual eggs on or even within the tissues of submerged water plants. Non-biting midges emerge in such numbers that their dancing swarms can sometimes look like columns of smoke. They supply a snack to many dragonflies and birds alike, yet still survive in numbers to lay their egg masses and repopulate the river once more.

FISH

For many people, fish symbolise the fascination of rivers, and they have long been used by man as a yardstick for river health. After all, fish place many exacting demands on a river if they are to find suitable spawning locations, nursery areas for the early stages, and both habitat and food to sustain them through the changing seasons.

A mayfly. Ephemera danica, *better known as the fisherman's mayfly, whose appearance in late May is enjoyed by both anglers and trout.*

In Britain as a whole, there are less than 60 species of freshwater fish, but in Dorset over 30 species are known from the freshwater and tidal reaches of our rivers. In fact, the River Avon is thought to have more species than any other British river. The Stour also has a diverse community of both salmonids and coarse fish, and whilst the Frome and Piddle have fewer coarse fish species, their salmonids are an important resource. All these rivers play host to Atlantic salmon and migratory sea-trout, and their sustainable management continues to exercise the minds of the Environment Agency, research workers and fishermen alike.

The Atlantic salmon in particular has a special fascination for both fishermen and naturalists. Sadly, the general concern over declining salmon stocks applies to southern chalk streams, as elsewhere. Scientists at the IFE River Laboratory have been monitoring the salmon runs on the River Frome for over 20 years and it is now apparent that stocks have declined. Whether this is due to problems within the marine or the freshwater phase of the life history of the salmon is still unclear. Long term rod catches of salmon within the river and commercial fishing in the estuary also show recent declines, although the numbers taken are a variable proportion of the total salmon run. Fish that have spent three winters in the sea enter the river in March and April, followed by two sea-winter fish in May-June and one sea-winter fish (grilse) in June-July. All these fish then move upstream to the main river spawning grounds in autumn, often at a time when the flow has started to increase. Evidence of a long-term decline of the three sea-winter fish which average around 10kg in weight is of particular concern. The management and monitoring of salmon spawning and nursery habitat is now a priority to ensure that adequate numbers of smolts make their way down to the sea. But how can the success of this operation be determined? A recent innovative technique developed by the IFE for counting these delicate fish automatically without the need to capture them is now providing another essential piece of the jigsaw in the quest to understand and reverse the decline of the salmon.

In addition to salmon and migratory trout, which favour the middle and lower reaches of the major chalk streams, the upper reaches of the Frome and the middle reaches of the Piddle also support good populations of brown trout. Further downstream on the Frome, below Dorchester, the grayling is an important member of the coarse fish community, but curiously, this species is absent from the Piddle. Although the upper sections of the chalk streams and their tributaries are generally regarded as trout streams, smaller fish including bullhead, minnow and stone loach are normally common and play a more significant role in the functioning of the river system. The bullhead for example has been shown to contribute over 80% of total fish production in some small streams.

Further downstream, coarse fish become more abundant, and fast-growing pike have ample opportunity to prey on species such as minnow and dace. Within the tidal reaches of the Frome and Piddle, several marine species also occur, including bass, thick and thin-lipped mullet, and flounder. On the Frome, these last two species have been found several miles upstream near the River Laboratory at East Stoke.

The River Frome, near East Stoke. The Frome and Piddle are both well-known for their salmon and sea-trout fishing, though in recent years stocks have been declining.

A kingfisher holding a bullhead. Bullheads are widespread throughout every river in the county, but kingfishers prefer the lowland rivers of central and eastern Dorset, particularly the Stour, whose steep-sided banks provide ample nesting sites.

A heron, photographed in the act of stabbing or taking a fish. The heron is increasingly common on all Dorset's rivers, but the biggest heronry in the county is in the middle of Poole Harbour on Brownsea Island.

Apart from salmon and migratory trout, a number of other fish move into our rivers from the marine environment to breed. They include the impressive sea lamprey and the smaller river lamprey, which are not true fish since they lack proper jaws. Both species occur in the Frome, Piddle, Stour and Avon, as does a third species, the diminutive brook lamprey, which remains in freshwater throughout its life and spawns on well-aerated river gravels. The smelt is a small migratory species, noted for its characteristic cucumber-like smell. Within Dorset, it has only been recorded in the lower Frome and, as yet, little is known of its detailed life history.

The River Stour is recognised as a fine coarse fishery, but salmonids are also common in the lower reaches of the main river and in some of the tributaries. Most of the salmon and migratory trout which move through Christchurch Harbour enter the River Avon, but salmon do spawn in the Stour itself below Blandford. However, the rod catch has been negligible for some years. The lower reaches of the Tarrant and the Allen are also used for spawning whilst migratory trout use the main river plus the River Crane and Mannington Brook in the Moors subcatchment. Brown trout occur in the lower reaches of the main river and its tributaries with the highest densities in the chalk tributaries, including the Crane and Allen. Unfortunately, the Allen has suffered from low flows in recent years due to groundwater abstraction, reducing the spawning and nursery habitat for salmonids in general.

A wide variety of coarse fish dominate the full length of the River Stour and include bleak, chub and barbel, which are absent from the Frome and Piddle. Roach and pike are common throughout the river, but grow more slowly than on the Frome and other chalk streams. Downstream of Wimborne the river is renowned for its population of barbel. Finally, the Stour, in common with the major chalk streams in Dorset, supports substantial numbers of eels, after they have completed their incredible journey, aided by the Gulf stream, from their breeding grounds in the Sargasso Sea.

BIRDS

Dorset plays host to a wide variety of birds. Rivers and their adjacent wetlands provide suitable conditions for a number of different species in the breeding season, on passage and through the winter. During the nesting season, vertical river banks, bankside vegetation and man-made structures such as bridges are all used as nest sites because they offer close proximity to a ready supply of food.

The dipper is an uncommon breeding resident in Dorset, because its specialist requirements are only met in the fast upland streams in the west of the county. Here it feeds underwater in shallow riffles, taking a variety of invertebrates, but with a particular preference for caddis larvae. Dippers pair and hold territory throughout the winter and start breeding early, sometimes rearing as many as three broods in well concealed nests built in natural or man-made crevices close to the water. Less specialised than the dipper and more widespread in Dorset is the grey wagtail, an elegant resident whose name describes the colour

of its back but fails to mention the black throat and bright yellow underparts which make the male so attractive in summer. Look for this long-tailed species near bridges, where its lively search for insects associated with fast-flowing rivers and streams adds interest to any riverside walk. For most of us, the sudden high pitched call and turquoise flash of colour as a kingfisher speeds past is always impressive. Kingfishers prefer the lowland rivers of central and eastern Dorset, and although they breed on our chalk streams, the Dorset Stour with its well-developed vertical earth banks provides optimal conditions for nesting and an abundant supply of small fish through the summer and autumn.

Where Dorset's major rivers and their tributaries have stands of bankside vegetation, a number of familiar water birds including the mute swan, moorhen, coot and little grebe nest in the margins. Although breeding adults eat a variety of submerged and emergent vegetation, newly hatched young supplement their diet with invertebrates to ensure a high protein diet.

In summer, well developed areas of marginal

OPPOSITE PAGE *A grey wagtail holding a mayfly.*

ABOVE *A dipper, an uncommon breeding resident in Dorset.*

BELOW *A little grebe on its nest, one of the birds that nest in the margins and backwaters of Dorset's rivers.*

ABOVE *The sedge warbler*

LEFT *The reed warbler. Both birds are summer visitors, building their nests in stands of reed or well-hidden in waterside vegetation.*

vegetation frequently support the ubiquitous sedge warbler, whilst the reed warbler is the most characteristic warbler of the common reed. It takes patience to distinguish the varied and energetic song of the sedge warbler from the more measured and repetitious strains of the reed warbler. In contrast, the cetti's warbler, has an unmistakable explosive song, which includes an insistent phrase somewhat reminiscent of its name. This resident species was first confirmed as a British breeding bird as recently as 1972, but can now be heard, and less frequently seen, at Radipole Lake and at a number of downstream locations on rivers which drain into Poole and Christchurch Harbours: the short riverside walk along the River Frome downstream of Wareham is one favoured location.

Many other birds which rely on insects for food are frequent visitors to rivers, where swarms of mayflies, caddisflies and true flies provide an easy feast. They include such summer migrants as sand martins, house martins and swallows. The hobby, an attractive falcon capable of taking martins, swallows and even swifts in flight, will also prey on dragonflies and damselflies, such as the distinctive banded demoiselle, before discarding their characteristic wings along the banks of some of our lowland rivers.

During spring and autumn passage, many different birds use rivers and adjacent wetlands for feeding and resting before their onward journey. In winter, the major river valleys become important wintering grounds for waders and waterfowl. One of the more remarkable visitors to arrive is the Bewick's swan, which can sometimes be located in the Lower Frome and Avon valleys after its long autumn retreat from the breeding grounds in arctic Russia. Winter can also produce the occasional surprise of an overwintering green sandpiper at a watercress bed, an elegant fish-eating goosander, and, in recent years, the sight of an egret stalking its prey from the water's edge.

MAMMALS

The three native mammals which occur on rivers in Dorset have very different feeding habits. The water shrew is a small but voracious predator on a wide range of invertebrates, amphibians and fish. It occurs in association with a variety of unpolluted streams and ponds with good cover. The maximum lifespan is about 18 months and each day its food consumption exceeds its own body weight, so a reliable source of food is a necessity. The water vole, alias 'Ratty' from *The Wind in the Willows*, feeds on a range of grasses and bankside vegetation on rivers, ponds and drainage ditches. Surrounded by food and with a rodent's ability to perpetuate its species, it used to be common on rivers in Dorset. However, the familiar sight of a vole sitting on its haunches and using its front paws to cram food into its mouth or paddling furiously to reach bankside safety has now become less frequent. The reasons are still unclear, but current concern is being translated into research and survey. Within Dorset a project to determine the current status of water voles, and what can be done to reverse the trend, is being co-ordinated by the Dorset Wildlife Trust, with help from the Environment Agency.

A water vole. Once common, numbers are declining. In Dorset, a research project is currently trying to establish the reasons, and what can be done to encourage their revival.

Otters remains a rare sight in Dorset. They have recently been reintroduced into the eastern part of the county, whilst a small number have always maintained a toe-hold in the west.

The third native species, the otter, is a very rare sight in Dorset, despite excellent stocks of fish and positive efforts by man to maintain suitable bankside habitat and construct artificial 'holts' on several rivers. The severe reduction in otter populations in England, primarily as a result of pesticides and loss of suitable habitat is well known, but there are encouraging signs that the small population in south-west England is expanding eastwards, and occasional reliable sightings of otters or their 'spraint' in Dorset give cause for cautious optimism.

The mink, a native of North America, escaped from British fur farms earlier this century and was first reported breeding in the wild in Devon in 1956. It is now widespread throughout Britain, including Dorset, but is rarely seen except by those who spend long hours on the river bank. It has more catholic tastes than the otter and takes fish, birds and mammals, including water voles – indeed some have suggested that the mink has contributed to the loss of the water vole from some river sites. Our rivers also provide food for bats in the form of flying insects. Thus, pipistrelles and Daubenton's bats take over as swallows and martins complete their day shift and go to roost.

QUALITY AND MANAGEMENT

Dorset is essentially a rural county with no big cities or centres of heavy industrialisation and it enjoys the benefit of high quality rivers with an impressive variety of wildlife. Nevertheless, the present state of our rivers has only been achieved through the concerted action and co-operation of many organisations over a long period, and much remains to be done. Man's impact on rivers is through management of the land within the catchment, and more directly through manipulation of the quantity and quality of the water in the river, the river habitats and its wildlife.

Within the county, farmers have made significant improvements in recent years in conserving soil and limiting run-off by fertilisers and farm wastes — all of which can easily result in siltation, enrichment and pollution of watercourses. Even so, there is a need for constant vigilance and advice on new procedures for minimising impacts, such as the adoption of buffer strips along the margins of streams and rivers. Forestry, mineral extraction and urban development take further substantial areas of land and an example of the impact of urbanisation on a river system can be found in the Moors River.

The lower Moors River was first notified as a Site of Special Scientific Interest in 1959 because of the exceptional richness of its dragonfly fauna and water plants. One dragonfly in particular, the orange-spotted emerald (*Oxygastra curtisii*), held pride of place, this part of Dorset being where it was first discovered and described in 1820. By the 1950s, the Moors River was the sole location for this species in Britain and excessive shading by bankside trees was reducing the amount of suitable habitat for the territorial males. Sadly, the final loss of this species in Britain is believed to be the result of accidental pollution caused by the Palmersford Sewage Treatment Works (STW), serving newly constructed housing estates. The last record for the orange-spotted emerald was in July 1963. Since then, housing development within the catchment has continued and strenuous efforts have been made to control run-off from the urban environment and from industrial estates. Finally, in 1992, effluent from the Palmersford STW, now operated by Wessex Water Services, was diverted by pipeline to the River Stour, since when the water quality in the Moors River has improved.

Increasing demand for water throughout Dorset is met through a combination of groundwater and surface water sources. Heavy utilization of the groundwater resources available within the chalk belt may alter flow regimes in winterbournes and perennial chalk streams, whilst removal of water from the lower reaches of the rivers reduces the flow available for dilution of effluents. Hence, difficult decisions have to be made. Groundwater abstraction from the River Allen to satisfy the Bournemouth and Poole conurbation with its increased requirements during the holiday season has resulted in low summer flows and biological impacts which include poor weed growth and the reduction of spawning and nursery habitat for salmonids. The upper and middle reaches of the River Piddle have also been affected by groundwater abstractions over a number of years, and the Environment Agency has devised Action Plans for each river to guide future management in an environmentally sustainable way in order to balance the needs of all legitimate users.

Many factors can contribute to the local or even the global extinction of species and amongst them, habitat loss and degradation, the spread of non-native species and over-exploitation are major components. Procedures for systematically recording habitat features and our understanding of their importance to wildlife have made significant advances in recent years. The natural features of rivers, together with management techniques such as dredging, weed cutting and the maintenance of banks, can all affect the physical nature of wildlife habitats, as can the quality and quantity of the water within the river. However, it is now becoming clear that rivers have great potential for recovery if sympathetic management based on understanding is applied.

The introduction of non-native species poses a different set of problems, some of which may be irreversible. The mink has already been mentioned, but another species from North America, the signal crayfish, is now posing a threat to our native white-clawed crayfish. The signal crayfish was first introduced into Europe because it grows more rapidly than some of the native species and is therefore valued by those rearing crayfish commercially. Unfortunately, it brought with it a fungal infection (*Aphanomyces astaci*), the so-called crayfish plague. Whereas the signal crayfish is plague-resistant, the infection has proved fatal to some of the European species. Introduction of signal crayfish from Sweden into Britain in 1976, when juveniles were distributed to several hundred sites, has led to the elimination of the native species from many rivers in southern and eastern England in the last 15 years. Within Dorset, the native white-clawed crayfish is now restricted to the rivers Piddle and Allen.

A number of invasive plants which were introduced in the last century have also spread along the banks of Dorset's rivers, to the detriment of the native vegetation. Himalayan balsam, Japanese knotweed, and even giant hogweed, have all been reported. Although at present they do not appear to be a major threat, careful monitoring is advisable, coupled with control where necessary.

Despite the many complex problems which remain to be resolved, our local rivers are a constant source of inspiration and pleasure, just as they were to past generations. There is now good reason to believe that, through the cooperative efforts of many organisations and individuals, they can be managed in an environmentally sustainable way, for the benefit and enjoyment of future generations.

An orange-spotted emerald dragonfly.

COMPLETING NATURE'S JIGSAW

The extensive loss of wildlife habitats since the end of the Second World War, (97% of our wildflower meadows, 75% of our heaths and 304,000 km of hedgerows throughout Britain), has left much of our wildlife restricted to nature reserves and smaller sites of nature conservation interest. Small and sometimes isolated pieces of 'waste' land not used for agriculture or such purposes as housing or industry have therefore become increasingly important sanctuaries for wildlife, completing the jigsaw of different habitats in Dorset.

Some species of native plants thrive under the particular conditions created by man's activities. These areas include roadside verges and hedgerows, so-called waste land at the edge of old gravel pits and quarries, parks and village open spaces, churchyards, walls and last but not least, gardens – in particular those gardened sympathetically with wildlife in mind.

CHURCHYARDS

Even amidst the bustle of Dorset's towns, its churchyards are places for quiet reflection, acting as tiny oases for a whole range of flowers and animals. Many of the medieval churches were built on open pasture land – the common fields

Spring on a Dorset verge. Bluebells, red campion and wild garlic line a lane near Bingham's Melcombe.

of the medieval manor, so that today their churchyards represent small patches of ancient meadow set within the improved farmland or town houses which surround them.

The grassland itself can span both damp and drier areas, furnishing the right habitats for a wide range of plants. The surrounding hedges and trees, particularly the traditionally planted churchyard yew, provide miniature woodland habitats, whilst the church walls and gravestones have become one of the commonest places to find lichens.

Churchyards are traditionally managed by regular mowing to maintain a tidy appearance. However, the nationally run 'Living Churchyard Project', set up to promote interest in wildlife in churchyards, has encouraged a re-assessment. Under the guidance of the Dorset Wildlife Trust nearly 50 churches have become involved. By mowing some areas less regularly a wide range of native plants are encouraged to flower, providing nectar for butterflies and other insects. If this is

carried out with care, and with neatly mown paths, the attractive appearance and wildlife richness of the churchyard can be enhanced.

Plants which frequently occur in churchyards throughout the county include important species that have been lost from many areas, such as cowslips, bird's-foot-trefoil, ox-eye daisy, bugle, rough hawkbit, lady's bedstraw and heath bedstraw. Trees provide shade for ground ivy, wood anemone and stinking iris. One churchyard has a glorious display of wild spring daffodils, whilst sharp-eyed visitors to another can find a succession of unusual flowers, including early purple orchids, spotted and twayblade orchids, dyer's greenweed, knapweeds, fleabane and the ubiquitous corky-fruited water-dropwort.

For lichens, the church walls and gravestones take the place of the bare rock surfaces found on coastal cliffs and other rock outcrops. Because of the considerable age of many church buildings and headstones, lichens have had centuries to

ABOVE *Wild daffodils and lichen on a gravestone in Holwell churchyard.*

LEFT *A lichen-covered gravestone in Studland churchyard.*

colonise them. The great variety of types of stone and surfaces enables different species to find suitable locations, each with its preferred conditions of prevailing shade and humidity. One rare species only occurs on crumbling lime mortar, and is in danger of extinction every time repairs are carried out. Many lichens develop in circular patterns and take about 100 years to cover a patch 10 centimetres in diameter. So far nearly a hundred Dorset churchyards have been surveyed for lichens: a quarter have over seventy different types, whilst five have more than a hundred species.

ABOVE *Heath spotted orchid and corky-fruited water-dropwort in a north Dorset churchyard.*

RIGHT *A black poplar outside the recently-restored White Mill, Sturminster Marshall. By the 1970s the black poplar was a largely forgotten tree, and only a few thousand were thought to survive. Those in Dorset include a pair at Hazelbury Bryan that rooted from stakes, and a line planted in 1979 along the banks of the Stour at Sturminster Newton.*

A wren 'spring-cleaning' by carrying a dropping from its nest. Wrens regularly nest in old farm buildings and barns, often building their domed nest of moss, grass and leaves in a hollow or crevice. Another favourite nesting site is a woodstack.

WALLS

Buildings and walls can provide important wildlife habitats. Although sadly less often seen nowadays, the common lizard still basks on dry stone walls, while the slow-worm finds a home under stones at the base. A handful of plants are adapted to obtain their supply of moisture from small cracks in brickwork pointing. A number of mosses and small ferns such as the delicate maidenhair spleenwort, black spleenwort and wall rue, are found in damper localities. Some small flowering plants are found only on walls, the most common being ivy-leaved toadflax, the introduced yellow corydalis, and red valerian. Less common are the charming small rue-leaved saxifrage and a relic of old cultivation, cornsalad, another member of the valerian family. In the north and west of the county, attractive spikes of wall pennywort, and shining cranesbill, both aptly named from the character of their leaves, can also be found. On old walls in some villages there are occasional plants of the original wallflower, surviving from early introductions.

HEDGEROWS AND VERGES

The unspoilt character of much of the Dorset countryside, with its winding lanes and network of minor roads, means that it still has considerable lengths of roadside verges and hedges rich in wildlife. For the motorist, they are perhaps the most visible habitat in the county. Many act as corridors along which animals can move and seed be dispersed, often linking other areas, such as woodlands, gardens and village greens. The value of roadside hedgerows and verges to wildlife has been increasingly recognised over the past few years. As hedges were grubbed out in the 1960s and 70s and fields enlarged, less space remained for once common plants, insects, birds and mammals. Surviving roadside hedges and the accompanying verges have become almost their only refuges in some areas, and this despite the increasing number of roadside casualties.

Some of our roadsides present a mosaic of colour throughout the year. A succession of flowering and fruiting plants, shrubs and trees all provide valuable food and shelter for insects, birds and small mammals. In effect, hedges are linear woodlands. Woodland ferns, such as hart's tongue, male and lady fern, flourish in the damp at their base. Fronds of polypody can sometimes be found growing out of old wood and the top of hedge banks. Patches of primroses welcome the spring, followed by red campion, bluebells, greater stitchwort, the aptly named 'jack-by-the-hedge' and, in some places, yellow archangel and ramsons, with its strong, characteristic smell of garlic. If you are lucky, you may see a patch of early purple orchid, which has a lovely old Dorset name — 'Granfer-griggle-sticks'. In midsummer, ox-eye daisies, hedgerow cranesbill and a variety of vetches add welcome splashes of colour.

Traditional hedge cutting and layering by hand have mostly given way to slashing or flailing by machine. The results can look unsightly and damaging, but, as long as the work is carried out in winter, after the berries have been eaten by birds, but before nesting, hedge management by machines does little lasting damage and does help keep the hedge growth healthy. Nevertheless, the revival of the ancient craft of hedge laying in some parts of the county is welcome.

Road verges are inseparable from the adjoining hedges. Some years ago the Dorset Wildlife Trust started a project to record the verges of greatest interest to wildlife, paying particular attention to less common plants. It now has a register of over a hundred prime verges, varying in length from 10 metres to 2 kilometres. Dorset County Council has been notified of these sites and manages them in co-operation with the Trust. They are clearly marked to enable verge-cutting contractors to follow specific advice about when to cut, allowing rarer plants to seed. Plants that benefit from this treatment include the rare narrow-leaved lungwort, which grows locally in the south-east of the county, spiny restharrow and the lizard orchid, our largest native orchid, which although rare has the slightly annoying habit of appearing in surprising places: one small colony continues to defy the traffic on a narrow verge two metres from a busy main road. The road verge

Our largest native orchid, the lizard orchid, on a roadside verge near Lytchett Matravers.

Wood anemones at the foot of an old laid hedge at Kingcombe Meadows.

A little owl about to land on its nest with an orange underwing moth in its beak. Because the little owl flies by day as well as at night, it can often be seen, usually in light woodland or open countryside. It usually nests in a tree-hole, but will also hatch out its brood of three to five nestlings in a wall, building, quarry or gravel-pit.

project needs constantly updating as local conditions change, and regular information on the health of the verges is crucial.

Some verges have become enriched by hedge cuttings and fertilisers used in adjacent fields. This may be responsible for the noticeable increase in the white drifts of cow parsley, which has the attractive local old name of Queen Anne's Lace. Other plants, such as comfrey, also benefit from high nutrient levels in the soil.

Other verges, particularly on the drier sand and gravel in the south-east of the county, suit some of the rarer smaller vetches and clovers, such as hare's foot clover and the aptly-named bird's foot clover, with its claw-like seed pods. Early autumn sees the emergence of members of the compositae, or daisy family, including fleabane, and, on one or two sites, the much rarer blue fleabane.

The county also has a number of unusual heathland verges in the south, where plants requiring an alkaline soil can surprisingly be found a few metres from heather and other associated acid-loving plants. This unusual combination is thought to be due to the use of limestone or chalk, which was originally laid down as hardcore for tracks over the soft peaty soils on parts of the wet heath. Plants that can be found on these verges include bee and pyramidal orchids, kidney vetch and dropwort. The margin of the Ferry Road between Studland and Shell Bay is an excellent example.

ARABLE FIELDS

Wild plants generally thrive where the soil is unbroken, but there are species which only germinate and flower after the soil has been disturbed. Such conditions arise naturally where landslips occur, in the wake of ploughing, and where earth has been moved, for example during road construction. With the intensive use of fertilisers and herbicides in modern farming many of these plants, often referred to as arable weeds, have become exceedingly rare. Many are small, and their attractions only become apparent when studied close-up, but they represent an important addition to the diversity of Dorset's flora.

Approximately 50 such plants have been found in the county. Some, such as the knotweeds and oraches, seen in cornfields after the harvest, are resistant to certain herbicides and have survived reasonably well. Others have seeds that remain dormant for many years. Who has not been delighted by the sudden sight of part of a field unexpectedly glowing red with common poppy? Our enjoyment is the farmer's misfortune, as it indicates that the particular area has escaped the application of expensive herbicide! Less common smaller poppies, such as prickly poppy, are

Prickly poppy growing on the edge of a cornfield near Briantspuddle.

amongst a group of plants that usually survive purely by luck on field edges occasionally missed by sprays. They include two charming members of the figwort family, sharp and round-leaved fluellen, and the intriguingly-named bellflower, Venus's looking-glass.

Sadly, many others are exceedingly rare, and a few are possibly extinct in Dorset, including the beautiful blue cornflower and pink corn cockle. The bright red pheasant's eye survives on one field margin in Purbeck, and the yellow corn marigold continues to flower in fields close to the River Frome. But the prospects for these arable wild flowers are brighter now than for many years, as increasing numbers of farmers are realising the importance of conservation and leaving broad strips of uncultivated land between field boundaries and their crops.

RAILWAY TRACKS

Railways tracks, particularly disused ones, provide a valuable habitat for a range of relatively rare plants, such as the pale and small toadflaxes. The embankment of the old railway line bordering the Dorset Wildlife Trust Powerstock Common Nature Reserve is an exceptionally good example of a man-made but undisturbed habitat that has evolved into rich grassland, with characteristic plants like dyer's greenweed, rock rose, spotted orchid, and quaking grass.

GARDENS AND PARKS

The importance of gardens for wildlife in our increasingly urban environment has gradually been recognised. All but the neatest and most drastically tidied gardens provide a habitat for a surprisingly large variety of plants and animals. Provision of bird feeding tables, nesting boxes and roosts in strategic places supplement natural food and cover. Compost heaps, leaf litter and piles of old logs provide shelter for insects, toads, slow-worms and hedgehogs. Garden ponds attract many kinds of invertebrates, including dragonflies and damselflies, as well as providing breeding places for frogs and newts.

Gardeners can easily get advice if they wish to garden in a 'natural' style that encourages conservation. To help, the Dorset Wildlife Trust is creating a demonstration garden at Preston near Weymouth. It was started in 1992 on a plot of land which had little wildlife interest but adjoined a large garden centre. It has been designed in two parts. The first is a small garden complete with borders and planted with wild plants such as teasel and eight-feet-high spikes of greater mullein, but also with garden plants like buddleia, perennial geraniums and sedum, all of which provide nectar for butterflies and other insects. A small pond, rockery and herb garden add variety. A hedge of native species has been planted, which after only three years already forms a protective shelter. The rest of the site is being developed to display a range of natural habitats, including a large pond, an open field and an area of native coppice trees. The field has already shown how a wide range of plants, like the local grass vetchling, can naturalise and spread to make pleasant summer displays capable of attracting butterflies, grasshoppers and other insects. As with the churchyards and roadside verges, timing grass cutting to ensure-optimum conditions for wildlife is important.

A spotted flycatcher. Spotted flycatchers arrive in Dorset in mid-May from their winter homes in Africa and northern India, often nesting on a creeper-covered trellis or house.

Finally, there are the many parks in Dorset's towns, which provide enjoyment for those who walk in them, and a broad mixture of habitats for wildlife. The traditional formal flower beds and closely-mown grass are gradually giving way to a more relaxed approach to park management, which encourages wild areas. Poole Park is outstanding. Its lakes attract numerous wildfowl, which in turn allow children and the townspeople to come into contact with wild creatures. The trees surrounding its open grass provide shelter and food for birds and the smaller mammals. Those unable to travel to the remoter nature reserves in the county will find much wildlife to enjoy in Dorset's parks.

Grass vetchling, one of the local flowers now flourishing in the Dorset Wildlife Trust demonstration garden near Weymouth.

A pair of common toads confront the camera. Gardens provide increasingly valuable refuges for frogs and toads.

EIGHT

NATURE CONSERVATION

THE DORSET SCENE

Even though an enormous amount has been lost, Dorset is still rich in natural resources. Few natural habitats have escaped disturbance in one form or another, and naturalists, concerned at the wildlife losses, have risen to the challenge of saving and restoring Dorset's wild places. Individuals, voluntary and statutory bodies, councils and industry are now working together to save the county's wildlife for future generations to enjoy. The last thirty years have seen great progress in this task, often using practical management techniques specially formulated for helping wildlife. There are so many excellent examples of nature conservation in Dorset it is an impossible task to give credit to them all, but this chapter is intended to provide an insight into how some of the problems are tackled.

Conservation usually starts by protecting natural areas by legislation, advice or purchase for management as nature reserves. Owners of some of Dorset's best wildlife habitats, such as the Dorset Wildlife Trust, the Royal Society for the Protection of Birds and the National Trust, work closely with the government's statutory advisers on nature conservation, English Nature, who in 1954, then known as the Nature Conservancy, declared Dorset's first National Nature Reserve at Hartland Moor. Now there are eight National Nature Reserves, and English Nature have

Golden Cap from the National Trust heathland at Stonebarrow Hill.

scheduled 140 Sites of Special Scientific Interest in Dorset (totalling 18,800 hectares), involving staff liaising with nearly 1,000 landowners.

In the early 1990s the Dorset Wildlife Trust embarked on a project to register all the remaining sites of interest which were not significant enough to be SSSIs. These Sites of Nature Conservation Interest (SNCI) have grown into one of the Trust's most valuable projects. It now has a register of nearly 1,200 sites which have been visited by SNCI staff, who provide advice to landowners and help in obtaining grant aid. As the register includes over 650 landowners and nearly 10,000 hectares of land the project is proving to be an important and healthy link between conservationists and the farming community.

In 1962 the Dorset Naturalists' Trust took over its first nature reserve by leasing the northern half of Brownsea Island from the National Trust. The Naturalists' Trust is now the Dorset Wildlife Trust, and today it runs about 40 reserves, funded by donations, grants and sponsors. Specialist groups such as Butterfly Conservation and the Woodland Trust have also flourished, and increasingly farmers and foresters are incorporating wildlife conservation into their work.

A group of sandwich terns on the Brownsea Island lagoon.

From the outset naturalists realised that practical work was needed to reverse the damage of neglect or mismanagement. Enthusiastic scrub bashing has gradually been distilled into organised work steered by well-researched management plans using volunteers reinforced by trained staff and contractors. Sites are now being managed as well as current knowledge and resources allow.

Conservationists now recognise that many habitats are the result of past human activity — farming, forestry, reed cutting, mineral working, etc — and increasingly these traditional methods are incorporated into the running of the reserves.

COAST AND MARINE LIFE

The need for the protection of shorelines against erosion at Hengistbury Head, and the dune system of the National Nature Reserve at Studland, highlights the fragile nature of coastal habitats, especially so close to large populations. Human disturbance has an impact on beach nesting birds: the ringed plover rarely breeds in Dorset now and oystercatchers only succeed in the quietest reaches of Poole Harbour. Important coastal tern colonies only survive on protected sites such as Chesil Beach and Brownsea Island, where continued work by two different owners has transformed the fortunes of these delightful birds.

Chesil Beach and the Fleet are unique. Over the last thirty years the Ilchester Estate has progressively taken more steps towards conserving their wildlife, funding the Chesil Beach and Fleet Nature Reserve. The Dorset Wildlife Trust was instrumental in starting summer wardening to protect the colony of little terns that nest on the shingle, and the Estate now employs a warden and runs an Information Centre. Little terns seem to wish ill-luck upon themselves. They nest close to the water in a highly exposed position on bare shingle, and are prone to disturbance by storms, walkers, and foxes. Despite the hazards, up to 50 pairs successfully nest in a wardened fenced area of the Beach.

Tern protection has also been a priority on Brownsea Island. In the early 1960s only a few pairs of common terns nested on the Brownsea lagoon. To improve the breeding numbers Operation Sea Swallow was launched in 1963 when the construction of artificial gravel islands was started. Though only a few square metres in size, these create ideal conditions for the terns. By 1967 42 pairs were nesting, protected from spring flooding by their new islands. In 1973 they were joined by sandwich terns, the first time this species had ever nested in Dorset. Following more island building, and the fitting of an electric pump to control the flooding in 1994, record numbers of terns nested on the lagoon in 1996. The 141 pairs of sandwich terns and over 160 pairs of common terns made the numbers nationally important, whilst the sandwich tern colony is now the most westerly in southern England.

Poole Harbour has long been recognised for its importance to wildlife, and is a Site of Special Scientific Interest (soon to become a Special Protection Area). Poole Borough Council has declared Parkstone Bay a nature reserve, helping emphasize how important for wildlife, especially birds, the harbour's shores and mudflats really are. A working group discusses all the relevant issues, and the Harbour Commissioners have developed an Aquatic Management Plan in an attempt to allow those who use the Harbour to enjoy it with as little effect on wildlife as possible.

The Harbour Gull Group was formed to protect the interests of one of Britain's rarest nesting birds, the Mediterranean gull, which nests on an isolated island in the harbour. The harbour's birdlife is remarkable, and is regularly studied by the members of the Dorset Bird Club, who organise monthly counts as part of a national initiative.

Other coastal birds are also at risk. Those nesting on the Purbeck cliffs were once susceptible to disturbance from climbers, but since the 1970s the County Council and the climbing clubs have liaised to restrict activities where guillemots and razorbills nest. To further strengthen the need for coastal conservation the Dorset Wildlife Trust employs a full-time warden at the Purbeck Marine Wildlife Reserve at Kimmeridge Bay. Here an understanding of the need for conservation is fostered by guided tours, a unique underwater nature trail, an underwater camera, and the aquaria in a visitor centre.

HEATHLANDS

The creation of Hartland Moor as a National Nature Reserve should have heralded the wiser use of Dorset's heathland, but it continued to be lost to farming or building. One minor compensation was that more sites were declared as National Nature Reserves: Morden Bog in 1956, Studland Heath in 1962, Holton Heath in 1981, Stoborough Heath in 1985 and Holt Heath in 1988. All heathland is now considered important, and English Nature's National Lowland Heathland Programme has helped encourage landowners to manage their heaths to improve the wildlife.

The cessation of traditional occupations such as grazing, turf cutting and controlled burning bring about natural changes which threaten heathland wildlife. New activities such as motor cycling, uncontrolled fires, and erosion present different problems. The spread of bracken, gorse, birch and pines, and the poor age structure of the heather, all contribute to the decline in diversity of the heather stands, creating less than ideal conditions for heathland specialists such as Dartford warblers, sand lizards and solitary wasps.

To reverse these changes scrub and bracken has to be removed before new areas of heather growth can be created. Some is cleared by hand, especially small pines, but bracken is usually sprayed. The methods for improving the age structure of heather include mechanical cutting and controlled burning, and on the larger sites there is a strong movement towards the reintroduction of traditional forms of grazing. Grazing creates small bare areas for insects such as solitary bees and digger wasps, helps the establishment of rare heathland plants, particularly annuals, and holds back the purple moor grass in the wet heaths.

The Dorset Wildlife Trust's first heathland reserve was Cranborne Common, which it leased from the Hatfield estate in 1963. Pony grazing has been tried to tackle the spread of purple moor grass and, with the help of grants from English Nature, further grazing may be implemented to encourage the growth of cross-leaved heath and reverse the spread of invasive plants over barer areas, a cause of the decline in marsh gentian, marsh clubmoss, and the loss of pale butterwort. The aim is to introduce grazing to all Trust heathland sites where practical.

In 1994, aided by English Nature's Wildlife Enhancement Scheme, the National Trust started grazing Hartland Moor using Exmoor ponies and 50 Red Devon Cattle. The cattle are grazed from May to November, the ponies all the year round. Eventually the whole area, including associated fields from two linking farms, will be grazed, extending the heath to 650 hectares. This is no mean feat — already approximately 15,000 metres of fencing and four cattle grids have been installed — and the funding from English Nature has been essential.

The restoration of heath from grassland means reducing soil fertility. This is achieved by applying ammonium sulphate to counteract the lime applied by past farmers and reducing the potassium and phosphate content. This is followed by silage cutting and light grazing. Other areas of Hartland Moor have been experimentally ploughed to expose dormant heather seeds.

After the Second World War foresters unwittingly allowed precious heathland to fall victim to ranks of conifers. Attitudes have since changed, and English Nature's Holton Heath National Nature Reserve is a good example of heathland restoration from coniferous woodland. To expose the sandy soils to the light, blocks of trees have been felled, encouraging heather growth and linking up remaining pockets of heath. The few trees deliberately left add to the site's scenic value (which includes glorious views of the northern

end of Poole Harbour), and provide diversity for the birdlife. Some have become song perches for nightjars, and in 1996 two pairs of woodlarks nested along with six pairs of Dartford warblers.

The RSPB Arne reserve was formed in response to the bad winters of 1961 to 1963, which reduced the Dartford warbler population on the Arne peninsula to only two pairs. Though the heathland was purchased to help the warblers the RSPB manage the reserve for all its wildlife. The larger the area, the more likely is this strategy to succeed, and the RSPB have continued to enlarge the reserve to its present size of over 500 hectares.

To survive winter snow Dartford warblers need mature heather and gorse to provide insects to feed on. To encourage this diversity the RSPB have created a mosaic of different aged heath, mirroring its traditional structure. This was achieved by controlled burning. Within about eight years gorse gives winter protection to Dartford warblers; after twenty-five heather will hold snow. Where burning is impractical, a forage harvester is used, which has the added benefit of harvesting seed that can be used elsewhere.

Though the trend is to manage habitats to benefit all wildlife, some conservation groups concentrate on just a few species. The destruction of the Dorset heaths lead to many of Britain's best reptile sites being lost at an alarming rate. The British Herpetological Society became active; fighting planning applications, leasing areas for management, and finally buying a reserve at Trigon.

To continue the work the Herpetological Conservation Trust was formed in 1989 and it now manages over 1000 hectares on reserves at St. Catherine's Hill near Christchurch, Hampreston, Parley, and Great Ovens at Sandford, and in conjunction with Forest Enterprise at Gallows Heath. Firebreaks and bare sandy areas for reptile basking and egg-laying sand lizards have been created, south facing slopes protected. The special needs of reptiles demonstrate the conflicts that management can bring: burning is thought to be destructive, and some species like

The heath in full colour. Bell heather, ling and dwarf gorse at the Dorset Wildlife Trust Tadnoll Nature Reserve.

mature heather on dry heath, making grazing less beneficial.

Conflicts are not rare on heathlands. Controversy surrounded Canford Heath in the 1980s when Poole Borough Council wanted to develop part of it. This became a classic case of housing threatening a specialised wildlife habitat, which finally ended in a large chunk of the southern part being lost to housing. Despite a major fire in 1997, the situation is no longer so bleak. The Council has its own countryside management team, who now safeguard the heath against rubbish being dumped, administer grazing of two-thirds of the remainder, and restore damaged heath by planting and laying turves. The involvement of local people inspired the forming of a Heathwatch team to help prevent fires, and in 1995 English Nature gave the Council their SSSI Award as an excellent example of a conservation-based countryside service with flexible ideas.

Poole Borough Council also manages Ham Common on the shores of Poole Harbour and owns 5 hectares of heath and pond in Parkstone called Alder Hills Nature Reserve. In 1991 the latter was leased to the Dorset Wildlife Trust as their first urban nature reserve. Although small, its rich wildlife includes a colony of sand lizards. Dorset County Council manages the heaths and woodlands of Avon Heath Country Park and East Dorset District Council manages Dewlands Common and St. Stephens Castle, both designated Local Nature Reserves. This marrying of nature conservation and countryside recreation is a successful formula for well-managed less sensitive sites.

Industry has also helped conserve Dorset's heath. BP has incorporated heathland restoration along their pipeline route from the Wytch Farm oilfield and created a 26 hectare conservation area on the Goathorn peninsula, where they have felled conifers, seeded bare ground with cuttings and planted heather turves. The Dorset Wildlife Trust has been helped by ARC, who leased and eventually sold the Trust a heathland reserve at Higher Hyde. It has a charming mix of old gravel workings and associated ponds, sallow woodland, and wet and dry heath and is managed by a Trust volunteer team. Further west the Ministry of Defence is responsible for large areas of heath at Lulworth and Bovington. Special routes are now used by tanks crossing the heath, and a management plan has been adopted for the conservation of the Lulworth Ranges. Ponds are an integral part of heathland ecology, supporting specialised dragonflies. Twenty-four species are found on the ranges, five of them nationally rare, and restoration work on the ponds at Lulworth gained it 'The Sanctuary' award in 1995.

GRASSLANDS

The traditional grazing and hay cutting which encouraged the rich mix of wildflowers, insects and birds on Dorset's downlands, meadows and pastures have been exchanged for more intensive methods. Artificial fertilisers, new grass mixes, drainage and ploughing have all played their part. The unique wildlife of the county's ancient grasslands owed its origins to grazing and haycutting, and if left unmanaged the downs and pastures would soon revert to woodland. Thus attempts to save their unique flora and fauna are now based on the farming methods which once sustained them.

The Dorset Wildlife Trust has long been concerned about protecting grassland, starting in the 1960s by managing parts of Hod Hill and Hambledon Hill. For years the Trust controlled only a few scraps, but it has gradually secured larger sites: chalk downland at Greenhill Down and Fontmell, limestone grassland at Townsend, Swanage, neutral grassland at Powerstock Common, and the 164 hectares of neutral and chalk grassland at Lower Kingcombe, an outstanding site purchased in 1987 after a hugely successful appeal.

Lying within the West Dorset Area of Outstanding Natural Beauty, the Kingcombe Meadows Reserve is mainly ancient unimproved pastures and meadows and thick hedges. The use of traditional farming methods, and the absence of pesticides and artificial fertilisers, make it rich in flowers and insects. The varied geology creates acid bogs and calcareous and neutral grasslands which can support a staggering 150 species of plants.The reserve has a full-time warden and a stockman who organise the grazing and haycutting on traditional lines, varying it to suit the demands of the wildlife. 110 hectares are grazed by local cattle (Hereford-Friesian crosses) resistant to the Red Water disease likely in the area. Their calves are born in March and April and put out to graze until November. By grazing or cutting the sward there is no build-up of grasses to choke the

wild flowers. The calves are sold at six months, and the rest of the herd (62 in 1996, including 36 Galloways) are left to graze until December, when the ground becomes too wet and prone to damage by trampling. The choice of Galloways is important. Their light weight means they do less damage to the ground. They also graze the whole sward, unlike the more selective Friesians, and can remain outside throughout the year. A flock of Beulah sheep graze alongside Kingcombe's cattle, producing about 140 lambs a year. Six of the Reserve's meadows are annually cut for hay, providing over 2,000 bales for winter feed for the cattle or sale. Many dislike seeing the taller flowers being cut in their midsummer prime, but without regular hay cutting the flora of the meadows would be replaced by coarser growth.

The management of a working farm like Kingcombe is a real challenge for a voluntary body like the Dorset Wildlife Trust. The reserve is registered organic with the Soil Association, leading to an annual inspection to ensure no fertilisers are used. The responsibilities of animal husbandry and estate work are enormous. The sheep have to be shorn, trimmed, vaccinated and

Green-winged orchids in flower in traditionally grazed meadows at Colehill, near Wimborne.

Hedge-laying at Kingcombe Meadows.

Blackthorn in blossom on the north slopes of Eggardon Hill. Marginal unimproved slopes such as these support a wide variety of insects, particularly butterflies.

sprayed. Fencing is required, hedges are laid on a 6 to 8 year cycle. Barns and handling facilities have been built and water provided to the fields – all supplied by the Trust and its sponsors, helped by Countryside Stewardship Grants. Running a farm nature reserve with the sensitivity its wildlife requires and the commonsense demanded by livestock is a major achievement for the Trust.

Grasslands support a whole range of insects not found in other habitats, and its destruction has brought many to the brink of extinction, particularly butterflies. For example, Britain is a major European stronghold for the marsh fritillary, but changes in agricultural practices and site fragmentation are leading to its decline. It breeds on small patches of rough grassland containing their food-plant, devil's bit scabious. A 10 to 15 cm high sward to protect overwintering larvae from the cold is also crucial. At the Trust's Bracketts

Coppice reserve there is a small central meadow with a strong marsh fritillary population. To prevent scrub encroaching on the grass, strips are now cut by a tractor and raked in the winter when the butterflies' larval webs are lowest in the grassland.

The Trust's reserve at Powerstock Common is much bigger – a fascinating mix of ancient woodland, old grassland and modern conifer plantations. Its size makes the reserve robust enough for species to move around and take advantage of the diversity of habitats. Since 1975 the Trust has been restoring the reserve by felling conifers and recreating the grassland. Initially this was cut for hay, so the stumps had to be removed, but grazing with cattle from Kingcombe now means they can be left to rot. The cattle keep the grass sward in the right condition for marsh fritillaries, and have helped improve the balance of the flora.

Butterflies are a feature of limestone and chalk grasslands, but their requirements vary. Close grazing early in the year encourages sheep's fescue grass, which in turn attracts the silver spotted skipper. The silver spotted skipper is only found at 14 sites in Britain, and only on Fontmell Down in Dorset. They lay their eggs on the underside of sheep's fescue, but the grass tufts have to be just the right length. The absence of grazing in early August then produces succulent leaf tips for the young caterpillars to feed on. Other species are just as fussy. Adonis blues need

An Adonis blue butterfly.

warm sunny south-facing slopes with a tight sward. Duke of Burgundy fritillaries breed at the scrub edges where cowslips grow. Successful downland management is a skilled task, and depends on getting the balance right between sward height, scrub growth and grazing pressure.

There are two other superb calcareous grassland sites near Blandford, Hod and Hambledon Hills, both hill forts of great archaeological importance. The National Trust bought Hod Hill in the mid 1980s and manages about 32 hectares on it, grazing cattle during summer and sheep from October to January. Electric fencing protects areas of deeper grass on the western ramparts for the larvae of the marsh fritillary and its foodplant, and sheep are sometimes penned on the southern ramparts to create a short turf to benefit the adonis blue. A similar pattern takes place on Hambledon Hill, where ownership is shared between the Chisel Farm Estate and the Hawthorn Trust, while English Nature is responsible for safeguarding its conservation as a National Nature Reserve.

The limestone grasslands on the coast are equally important. Durlston Country Park dates from the Victorian period, but by the 1970s its downs were being eroded, cars and motorbikes were unrestricted, and climbing was disturbing the cliff-nesting birds. In 1973 it was bought by Dorset County Council and it became a Country Park officially recognised by the Countryside Commission. About one third is downland, one third hay meadows and one third woodland and undercliff, plus smaller habitats such as old quarries and drystone walls. The downland and meadows are of high quality, supporting early spider orchids, nit grass and adonis blue and Lulworth skipper butterflies. The meadows are species-rich and the cliffs possess a good range of coastal plants. The prominence of Durlston Head makes it an important bird and insect migration site, and the Information Centre boasts a monitor which receives pictures from a cliff-mounted camera trained on the summer breeding colony of guillemots (about 300 pairs) and a few pairs of

Cowslips and early purple orchids on Hambledon Hill, a National Nature Reserve.

razorbills. With its clifftop walks, high downland vistas and the cheering song of soaring skylarks, Durlston is an uplifting place to visit.

A site as varied as Durlston has to be managed as a mosaic of habitats: encroaching scrub may threaten downland plants, yet simultaneously provides essential cover for migrating and resident birds. Green-winged orchids, quaking grass and clouds of pale flax survive in the meadows due to an annual hay-cutting reducing competition from more aggressive species. Durlston is a good example of how conservation and recreation can co-exist. 400,000 people visit Durlston a year, and yet, by using nature trails, the wildlife is barely affected.

The maintenance of grassland for wildlife and for gunnery may seem a contradiction, but the grasslands around Tyneham and on the Lulworth Ranges owned by the Ministry of Defence have escaped the ploughing which has destroyed so

Sheep enjoying the view from the slopes of Eggardon Hill. Stock grazing is an essential means of maintaining open grasslands.

much elsewhere. There is a conservation management plan and the downs are grazed, but conservation is inevitably restricted by the demands of military training and the danger of shells. The experts on the Ministry's Conservation Committee have access to the ranges, providing it with a wealth of information on vascular plants, lichens and bryophytes, birds, and dragonflies – all of which helps build bridges between the MOD and conservationists, who see the Ranges as a major part of Dorset's natural heritage.

The National Trust own large tracts of grassland on the Purbeck coast, and at Godlingston Hill and Ballard Down. Their biggest problem has been the spread of gorse, which has been reversed by cutting and burning followed by grazing with cattle. In 1976 a scheme was devised on Ballard Down to restore arable fields to grassland by seeding with grasses and encouraging wild plants to colonise naturally. The National Trust also manages prime coastal limestone grassland sites at Dancing Ledge, Spyway Farm and Seacombe - where the spread of tor grass has been checked by 25 Exmoor ponies and cattle, both maintaining the traditional Purbeck landscape and encouraging plants like the early spider orchid.

Bournemouth Borough Council have also been tackling grassland conservation. Hengistbury Head is a unique site boasting heath, woodland, dunes, saltmarsh and acid grassland; over 530 plant species have been recorded and like Durlston it is an important bird migration point. Its grasslands have existed since Roman times and its attraction to visitors has caused serious erosion in the lower fields and near the cliffs, so the Council have devised a scheme of fencing and footpaths which, although not totally denying public access, has done much to benefit the wildlife and the Head's intrinsic archaeological value. The Double Dyke has dramatically improved, with a range of old grassland plants such as upright chickweed and hairy birdsfoot trefoil now showing, and skylarks and meadow pipits are now nesting there again.

WOODLANDS

Viewing the heavily wooded landscape from the summit of Hambledon Hill you might think Dorset's woodlands need no conservation. Yet contained in that panorama are several nature reserves which demonstrate why woods need to be managed for wildlife. Most of our small woods were run as coppice-with-standards. The periodic cutting of the hazel every 5 to 15 years created clearings, inspiring a profusion of spring and summer flowers in the first few years after coppicing, and in turn leading to a boom in birds, butterflies and other insects. To retain the community of plants and insects linked to coppicing the period of shade as the hazel regrows is equally important. Even now, some of the cyclical processes which determine our woodland wildlife are unclear, but retaining or restarting centuries-old traditional methods of management are essential.

Bracketts Coppice near Corscombe is an excellent example of how research can help woodland reserve managers in the future. Its 28 hectares are diverse: pedunculate oak, ash, hazel and birch, with old pasture and a stream. Because of their dramatic decline in the 1980s the priorities for conservation were the pearl bordered fritillary and the wood white. Dr Jeremy Thomas, a professional entomologist, advised the coppicing of 0.2 hectares of woodland per year on a 10 year cycle. This would open up the heavily shaded woodland which had more or less killed the foodplants of their caterpillars (violets for the fritillary and trefoil for the white) and changed the wood to the detriment of the adult butterflies. Dr Thomas found that the young coppice growth and patchy bracken kept the young pearl bordered caterpillars warm in the spring, ensuring their survival. Sadly the efforts to save them were too late, and both species had vanished from Bracketts by the early 1990s. However, much was learned, and the coppiced clearings are now home to small pearl-bordered fritillaries, silver-washed fritillaries, white admirals and garden and wood warblers.

Milborne Woods in May.

A small pearl bordered fritillary, one of the butterflies in the Dorset Wildlife Trust Bracketts Coppice Nature Reserve near Corscombe.

Butterflies are a useful indicator of the health of a wood: what is good for butterflies generally encourages other wildlife as well. The Dorset Wildlife Trust leases two other woodlands near Sturminster Newton, Girdlers Coppice and part of Piddles Wood, where the Bracketts experience was invaluable. By the late 1980s pearl-bordered fritillaries had died out in Piddles. They were reintroduced in 1993, six years after the resumption of coppicing. They now seem to be on the increase, and the woodland flora is vastly improved.

Butterfly Conservation's research has shown that of 20 colonies of pearl bordereds in Dorset in the 1970s only two now remain. A Species Action Plan has been devised based on maintaining the butterfly on clusters of sites where the populations can be mobile, as they used to be when woods were managed commercially. The ideal security would be to ensure that places like

Piddles and Girdlers Coppice are coppiced commercially again, which is beginning to happen, so that the butterflies are supported by a local economy rather than intensive conservation work.

In 1985 the RSPB bought Garston Wood in Cranborne Chase. It is a superb example of ancient woodland on calcareous soil where hazels were cut every 10 years to supply poles for thatching spars and hurdles, and the RSPB continue coppicing it today. Thirty species of butterfly have been recorded and the regrowing coppice attracts nightingales and nesting turtle doves. The RSPB warden makes dead hedges of the cut poles around the coppice clearings to keep deer from browsing; a problem throughout Dorset, including the Woodland Trust's Duncliffe Wood, where conifers have been felled to reinstate deciduous woodland, only to find serious deer damage follows.

Circumstances often change our preconceived ideas about conservation. A history of neglect, deer damage and the uncontrolled spread of rhododendron are familiar problems to the National Trust and the Dorset Wildlife Trust on Brownsea Island, where an unusual form of conservation woodland management is employed. Most naturalists have little time for Scots pines, primarily because they encroach on heathlands and support less wildlife than deciduous trees. Those on Brownsea Island are essential for the survival of Dorset's remaining red squirrel population, which feeds on the cones. The pine woodlands are surprisingly rich on the Island, supporting nesting herons, woodcock and nightjar, as well as bats and many insects.

Since 1963 the Trust has been clearing rhododendron on the northern half of Brownsea. After the 1990 storm when hundreds of important squirrel feeding trees were blown down, the Trust embarked on a system of clearance and fencing off deer and rabbit free areas. Scots pines growing in open conditions produce most cones, so woodland is thinned to provide about 100 to 200 trees per hectare and room for young trees to grow. The work has been much-praised, and in 1996 the

A woven hazel anti-deer fence round a newly-coppiced clearing in the RSPB's Garston Wood Reserve on Cranborne Chase.

Dorset Wildlife Trust was awarded the Forestry Authority's 'Centre of Excellence' award for red squirrel conservation and public access on Brownsea.

It must be said that woodland management is not just about felling trees — lichens and bryophytes on ancient trees depend upon their continuing long life. Veteran parkland trees occur at Lulworth Park and Kingston Lacy for example, and those in Melbury Park are pollarded to retain their traditional character. Ancient trees are particularly good for insects such as wood boring beetles, and standards in woodlands which are dead or contain a high proportion of dead wood are essential for wood wasps, tree creepers, owls and woodpeckers.

It would be unfair to ignore the contribution made by private landowners in looking after Dorset's wild places. Many farmers take great pride in their woodlands, hedges, grasslands and ponds, working closely with English Nature, the Farming and Wildlife Advisory Group, and the Ministry of Agriculture. There is no better example than a farm on the edge of the Blackmore Vale whose woods are coppiced, where thousands of trees have been planted, dormice are monitored, otters have been reintroduced on the river and the increase of breeding herons watched with great pride. Ultimately, the future of much of the countryside depends on the farming community.

WETLANDS

Despite centuries of land drainage and water abstraction Dorset still has some valuable wetland areas, though only a tiny proportion of its original water meadows, ponds and ditches, reedbeds and other wet areas still exist. Vast areas of farmland extend without any relief for our wetland wildlife and many streams dry out in the summer. Coastal wetlands are restricted by geology – the impenetrable barrier of Dorset's cliffs allows estuary conditions only in Poole and Christchurch harbours, and at Weymouth, where the impeded natural drainage of the Wey forms the Radipole and Lodmoor nature reserves.

Despite the losses to drainage excellent wet areas still exist, some of which are protected as conservation areas or as part of river systems, managed by the Environment Agency Catchment Management Plans. The rivers Frome, Piddle, Stour, Allen and Moors flow into the eastern harbours, and are straddled with water meadows, reedbeds, typha beds, carr and fen – even supporting an increasing otter population. Surviving patches of wet grassland support scarce wetland plants and insects, but mammals and birds need larger areas of suitable countryside, and their decline has been more serious. Snipe may winter in Dorset but generally none nest here now. The decline of the water vole, possibly linked to an increase in escaped mink, is largely due to the loss of lush riverside vegetation as fields are improved right to the water's edge.

Radipole Lake Nature Reserve has been leased by the RSPB from Weymouth and Portland Borough Council since 1976. Despite the pressures of an urban environment the reserve flourishes and has excellent facilities, including a reed-thatched visitor-centre, bird hides and paths leading to a scarce habitat - reedbeds containing the core of Dorset's bearded tit population, cetti's warblers and occasional overwintering bitterns. The reserve's future success depends on ensuring the continuity of good quality reedbeds, as a build-up of dead reed litter can lead to drying out and succession to woodland. To reduce this about 1 hectare of reeds are cut on a 7 year rotation, the dead reed being cut, raked and burnt. This also provides the diversity of age and structure required by the bearded tits and reed warblers. The bearded tits nest low down in the reed stands and like the cut areas for feeding; uncut reeds provide nesting space for summer visiting reed warblers and late pairs nest in the new growth. Scrub in the beds attracts nesting pairs of the scarce cetti's warblers, so it is encouraged along the path edges where they like to nest, but cut elsewhere.

Reedbeds require regular winter flooding to help the litter rot down. Radipole's urban location can make flooding from the River Wey excessive, posing an additional threat. The floodwaters are heavy with silt, which enriches the reedbeds with nutrients, accelerating reed growth and hastening natural succession to scrub, which ultimately can threaten the wildlife. The RSPB are also investigating whether introduced carp are having a detrimental effect on the aquatic ecology as they uproot plants, affect the water quality and eat the invertebrates enjoyed by wintering wildfowl. Managing nature reserves is rarely simple !

Reedbeds occur throughout Dorset in tiny areas in fields or strips along river banks, particularly around Poole Harbour and at Abbotsbury. Here you can find reed warblers, sedge warblers, cetti's warblers, bearded tits and wintering bittern, as well as water voles and the reed-feeding flame wainscot moth. Of the 20 or so hectares at Abbotsbury, half are still cut commercially for thatching. The rest is set aside for conservation, though a few acres are periodically burned to prevent litter build up. The Holton Lees Trust at Lytchett Bay owns extensive saline reedbeds on the edges of Poole Harbour, cut for thatching until recently, and in the Purbecks a Habitat Action Plan is being developed to help conserve the remaining beds.

Remarkably, Brownsea Island has an important wetland system which begins with a spring feeding two acid lakes, valuable for wintering pochard

Gulls amongst the reedbeds at the RSPB's Radipole Lake Nature Reserve, Weymouth.

and tufted ducks and breeding little grebe. It flows through alder carr and reedbeds and into a 28 hectare brackish artificial lagoon – just like a miniature river system. By removing encroaching rhododendron and other scrub, coppicing, ditching and creating pools, the Trust is developing the whole valley as one wetland system, even installing ditches and sluices to control water levels. Higher levels provide suitable feeding conditions for wintering snipe and water rails, whilst cutting corridors in the reed encourages reed warblers and adds to the diversity. The marsh-side rushy areas are much liked by water voles in winter, who exchange the dead winter reedbeds to feed on the rushes.

The Brownsea lagoon is of considerable importance to bird conservation. Shallow, muddy and brackish, it was cut off from the sea by a sea wall in the 1850s, and now contains saltmarsh, mudbanks and open water. Because it isn't tidal, it forms an important roosting area for many of the harbour's waders, and at high tide dunlin, oystercatchers, black tailed godwits, grey plover and curlew congregate in it from October to March. Many of the birds are in numbers of national importance: in recent years wintering avocets have increased to several hundreds, a stunning site for birdwatchers. Controlling the water level is vital. Winter rainfall can flood the lagoon, rendering it useless for wintering waders for weeks on end – a problem now solved by the installation of a submersible electric pump. Controlled by float switches, it can pump at 130 litres a second, automatically creating the ideal conditions for birds and the invertebrates they feed on. The lagoon has been transformed. In winter hundreds of waders now land on it daily, some such as redshank and black tailed godwit returning after many years, and terns can now nest without fear of spring flooding.

Wetland conservation does not need to be limited to nature reserves. As the most westerly chalk stream in Britain, the River Frome is in the process of being designated an SSSI. The river is rich in wildlife, with only occasional signs of damaging nutrient enrichment from farming or drainage. The designation includes semi-natural habitats alongside the river, including the beautiful fens and wet pastures at East Stoke and East Holme. The river's environs have already lost some of their breeding birds, like snipe and redshank, but others like kingfishers, reed and sedge warblers still flourish, and in the longer term new initiatives will hopefully expand the wet meadows to reverse the losses.

This sort of broad-based look at the countryside is the way forward. English Nature are currently trying a project in the Blackmore Vale to encourage the conservation of a wide range of natural habitats. Dorset County Council's countryside service have similar initiatives intended to bring local communities and their countryside together, one of which, the Stour Valley project, covers the 28 parishes that border the river, from its entry into the county in the north to its mouth in Christchurch Harbour. Another is the restoration of water meadows at Maiden Newton, where it is hoped to re-establish the old system of channels used to flood the meadows and once again graze them with sheep. This is a good example of linking people, history, landscape and nature conservation.

Dorset has been fortunate for more than forty years in having a major national Ecological Research Station at Furzebrook, near Wareham. The work of the scientists there has made a major contribution to our knowledge and understanding of the processes on which the work of nature conservation is now based. The Dorset Wildlife Trust in particular has benefited from their work and a number of the staff have been active in support.

The energy, commitment and imagination of Dorset's conservationists allows a sense of optimism. Much has been achieved, much is in safe hands. We must just hope that the lessons learnt so painfully in the past help us triumph over the inevitable threats brought by the future.

An over-wintering avocet in the lagoon on Brownsea Island.

INDEX

(NOTE: all plant and animal names begin with a small letter. All place names begin with a capital letter to enable easy separation)

NATURE RESERVES & WILDLIFE SITES

BBC   Bournemouth Borough Council
CBC   Christchurch Borough Council
DCC   Dorset County Council
DWT   Dorset Wildlife Trust
EDDC   East Dorset District Council
EH   English Heritage
EN   English Nature
FE   Forest Enterprise
MOD   Ministry of Defence
NT   National Trust
PBC   Poole Borough Council
PDC   Purbeck District Council
RSPB   Royal Society for the Protection of Birds
WPBC   Weymouth and Portland Borough Council
WT   Woodland Trust

The list on the pages that follow is of some of the best places in Dorset to enjoy wild plants and animals. Almost all are accessible to visitors, and most are in the care of conservation organizations or local councils. Please remember that thoughtless visitors can easily harm what they have come to enjoy, so keep any disturbance to a minimum. Cameras and binoculars should be all the equipment you normally need.

Do look out for notices and leaflets at the larger sites and follow the specific advice given. Many reserves have wardens willing to help you enjoy your visit and provide information. At a few there are Visitor Centres, viewing hides and trails.

Always take an Ordnance Survey Pathfinder or Landranger map with you on your visit. Remember that although a reserve may be managed by a conservation body the land may be privately owned. If in any doubt about access please stay on public rights of way as shown on the OS map.

Each year sees an ever-growing number of guided walks on reserves led by wardens and other local experts. Details are contained in the leaflets published by individual organisations and in the annual Dorset Countryside Book from Dorset County Council, which is widely available from shops, libraries and Tourist Information Centres. The programme detailed in the latter also includes special events and excursions, including boat trips from places like Poole Quay, Swanage, and Lulworth Cove.

Please note that this list is only a selection of the finest places to see wildlife. The descriptions are necessarily short; for more detail of the notable plants and animals to be found please see the main text, using the index to help you. Reserves in the care of the Dorset Wildlife Trust are highlighted.

The many coast and countryside walks in the county are not included in the list, but they do provide a wonderful opportunity for observing wildlife. Amongst the most notable are the Dorset Coastal Path, the Wessex Ridgeway, Brit Valley Way, Stour Valley Way and Wareham Forest Way. Places with an admission charge such as the Sea Life Centre at Weymouth and Purbeck's Blue Pool are mostly omitted, but they also offer much of interest to the naturalist. Courses, holiday activities and expertly led walks are offered by The Kingcombe Centre, Toller Porcorum, Dorchester DT2 0EQ and Leeson House Field Studies Centre, Langton Matravers, Swanage EH19 3EU.

ABBOTSBURY SWANNERY
SY 575840 PRIVATE
Ancient swannery south of Abbotsbury village on the shore of the Fleet lagoon. Opportunity to see nesting mute swans at close quarters. Views of the western end of the Fleet lagoon and Chesil Beach. Information Centre and warden. Open summer.

ALDER HILLS
SZ 063931 DWT
5 hectare urban reserve comprising a large lake, formerly a clay pit, a margin of carr woodland and slopes and ridges of heathland. Noted for reptiles. Access from Community Centre next to Sainsbury supermarket, Alder Road, Parkstone.

ARNE
SY 984885 RSPB
Large and varied reserve with extensive heathland, woodland and marshes bordering Poole Harbour. Outstanding heathland flora and fauna including Dartford warbler and nightjar. Also good for winter wildfowl, for waders, and birds of prey. Nature trail, bird hides, wardens and guided walks. RSPB car park at reserve entrance near Arne village, path to Shipstal Point.

AVON HEATH COUNTRY PARK
SU 125039 DCC/DWT
Country park south-west of Ringwood. Comprises separate North Park, South Park and Matchams View totalling 243 hectare. Heathland and coniferous woods. DWT protects 8 hectare of dry heath, especially for reptiles, as nature reserve. Visitor Centre, wardens, events, picnic sites and waymarked paths. Friends group. Main car park off south side of A31. Other car parks off Hurn and Boundary Lane.

BADBURY RINGS
SY 965030. NT
Iron Age hill fort on Kingston Lacy Estate north-west of Wimborne. Rich downland flora on the Rings and surrounding land. Good for orchids and butterflies. Crown of hill wooded. Two contrasting woodlands nearby (Highwood and The Oaks). Wardens, guided walks, events. Car park off B3082 Wimborne-Blandford road.

BALLARD DOWN & OLD HARRY
SZ 048812 NT
Steep downland slopes above Whitecliff Farm. Rough grassy cliff-tops between Ballard Head and Old Harry Rocks. Restoration of previously cultivated plateau. Good for chalk flora and coastal plants, butterflies and seabirds. Easily accessible on foot from Studland and Swanage (via Ulwell or Whitecliff Farm). Coastal path walk popular. Wardens and guided walks. Car parks in Studland (NT) or north Swanage.

BRACKETTS COPPICE
ST 514074 DWT
23 hectare of varied broadleaved woodland and neutral pasture. Outstanding for butterflies. Coppice management. Limited car parking. Access by permissive footpath.

BROWNSEA ISLAND
SZ 025882 NT/DWT
Poole Harbour's largest island (202 hectare). DWT manages nature reserve of 101 hectare on north side of island. This includes saltmarsh, lagoon, reedbed, lakes, woodland and carr. Notable for large heronry, nesting tern colonies and red squirrels. Visitor Centre in Villa. Bird hides, guided tours, self-guided walks and wardens. Other privileges for DWT members.

Southern part of island also rich woodland and heathland. Access April-end of September. Visit by boat from Poole Quay. Car parking nearby. Landing fee. NT Information Centre, shop and cafe at Quay. Can be combined with round Poole Harbour cruise to see birdlife.

CHARMOUTH HERITAGE COAST CENTRE
SY 365930
Excellent centre from which to explore beaches and landslip cliff areas between Golden Cap and Lyme Regis including Black Ven and The Spittles. Rich marine life and geological interest. Displays, wardens, guided walks and Friends. Safety advice on dangerous stretch of coast. Car park nearby.

CHESIL BEACH & THE FLEET
SY 568840-668754 PRIVATE
Famous shingle storm beach over 25km long, west of Portland. The Fleet, a sheltered brackish lagoon nature reserve lies behind. Beach good for shingle flora. Fleet exceptional for wildfowl and waders, including swans (see Abbotsbury Swannery above). Common and little tern colonies specially protected. Ferry Bridge area good botanically. Information and wardens. Beach can be dangerous. Car park nearby at SY 668753.

COOMBE HEATH
SY 862848 DWT
40 hectare of wet and dry heath dotted with several tumuli. Typical heathland flora and fauna. Access by bridleway. Parking at SY 859849.

CORFE CASTLE COMMON
SY 960810 NT
A large area of wildlife-rich grassland and scrub, much of it never ploughed, at southern end of Corfe Castle village. Access on foot from West Street car park or from road to Kingston.

CORFE MULLEN MEADOW
SY 980967 DWT
2 hectare flower-rich meadow noted for abundant green-winged orchids. Limited roadside parking.

CRANBORNE COMMON
SU 108118 DWT
45 hectare isolated block of heathland transitional in character between Purbeck and New Forest. Mainly humid and wet heath. Notable for plants and birds. Access by public footpath from Verwood or Alderholt.

DUNCLIFFE WOOD
ST 825225 WT
88 hectare mixed woodland on hilltop west of Shaftesbury. Ancient woodland site being restored to native woodland after previous part conversion to conifers. Limited parking. Foot access by track to west side of wood from minor road towards Stour Row south of A30, ST 816224.

DURLSTON COUNTRY PARK
SZ 032773 DCC/PDC
104 hectare coastal park near Swanage. Fine cliff walks with seabird colonies and coastal plants. Limestone grassland specially managed for conservation a notable feature. Scrub gives shelter for arriving migrant birds and old quarries add further variety. Butterflies especially good. Visitor Centre with displays, interactive video and HQ for Coastwatch project. Wardens, guided walks, events and Friends. Car park near Durlston Castle and Visitor Centre. Can also be reached on foot by coast path from Peveril Point, Swanage.

EAST STOKE FEN
SY 864866 DWT
4.5 hectare of Reedmarsh, wet woodland and oak copse on floodplain of River Frome east of Wool. View from public footpath alongside.

EGGARDON HILL
SY 540946 NT
19 hectare of chalk downland including half of the Iron Age hillfort. Rich turf. Good for butterflies. Access from A35 between Bridport and Dorchester on minor road through Askerswell. Limited parking in lay-by.

FERRYBRIDGE & SMALLMOUTH
SY 668761 WPBC
Rich area off A354 Portland road from Weymouth at junction of the Fleet/Chesil Beach and Portland Harbour including disused railway line. Warden and guided walks. Car park and Information Centre near Ferrybridge SY 668753.

FIFEHEAD WOOD
ST 775215 WT
20 hectare of ancient dry and wet woodland with oak and ash trees over hazel coppice. Damp-loving plants along streamside and ditches. Former osier bed at western end. Fine spring display of bluebells. South of A30 Shaftesbury-Sherborne road close to village of Fifehead Magdalen. Often wet underfoot. Limited parking in lay-by at east end of wood.

FONTMELL & MELBURY DOWN
ST 884176 NT/DWT
Outstanding chalk downland estate of over 300 hectare including Melbury Beacon ST 900193. DWT reserve of 57 hectare includes steep-sided coombe prominent in westward view from higher Blandford/Shaftesbury road. Major conservation site for chalk flora and fauna. Orchids and huge variety of butterflies are highlights. Scrub and woodland rich in birds. Access via public and permissive footpaths from small NT viewpoint car park at top of Spread Eagle Hill (ST 886187). Alternative parking at Compton Abbas airfield or in Fontmell Magna

village below reserve (one mile walk from A350 lower Blandford-Shaftesbury road to end of Springhead Trust grounds).

GARSTON WOOD
SU 004194 RSPB
35 hectare ancient traditionally coppiced woodland on Cranborne Chase. Coppice management revived but some parts left to mature as high forest. Excellent for birds such as nightingales and garden warblers, and for butterflies. Approach from Blandford-Salisbury road A354. One mile north of Sixpenny Handley. Small car park.

GIRDLERS COPPICE AND PIDDLES WOOD
ST 798135 DWT
Fine examples of oak woodland and hazel coppice. Rich in ground flora, butterflies and typical woodland birds. Girdlers Coppice (7 hectare) includes wet meadows by the River Stour. Access to Girdlers Coppice by permissive path (courtesy of the owner) from Fisherman's Car Park near Fiddleford Mill at ST 801135.

Piddles Wood (ST 797127) privately owned - access by public right of way only to this 17 hectare wood east of the A357 road just south of Sturminster Newton. Rear gate at ST 792127.

GODLINGSTON HEATH (STUDLAND)
See Studland Heath

GOLDEN CAP ESTATE
SY 4092 NT
810 hectare of hill, farmland, woodland, cliff, undercliff and beach including over 11km of coast and 40km of walking paths. Conservation management ensures varied wildlife. Superb meadows. Best access from Stonebarrow Hill up steep minor road from A35 by Newlands caravan site east of Charmouth. NT Information Centre and car parking at SY 384934.

GREENHILL DOWN
ST 792037 DWT
12 hectare of chalk grassland and coppice woodland. Wide range of flora and fauna. Scrub and a small pond add variety. Access by public footpath up hill from Hilton, north of Milton Abbas. Limited parking in village at ST 792037. Avoid obstructing access to church.

HAMBLEDON HILL
ST 845125 EN
National Nature Reserve of 74 hectare. Extensive chalk grassland varied in slope and aspect. Impressive Iron Age hillfort. Notable for flora and butterflies. Partnership of two owners (including grazing as part of an organic farm) with English Nature and English Heritage. Access to open areas of reserve but not to Yew Wood. Limited parking off Duck Street and Shaftesbury road near Child Okeford. Use footpaths and bridleways to reach hill.

HARTLAND MOOR & STOBOROUGH HEATH
SY 945855 NT/EN
353 hectare National Nature Reserve between Wareham and Corfe Castle. Superb dry heathland and valley bog draining into Poole Harbour. Areas of heathland restoration adjoin. Access from Soldiers Road off A351 south of Stoborough or from western end of Hartland Moor near Slepe Farm (EN offices) along old mineral tramway. Limited roadside parking.

HENGISTBURY HEAD
SZ 175907 BBC
100 hectare coastal headland on eastern edge of Bournemouth. Reserve includes woodland, grassland, heath, ponds and coastal habitats bordering sea and Christchurch Harbour. Staging post for migrant birds. Visitor Centre, trail, wardens. Car park at end of Broadway off Belle Vue Road, Southbourne.

HIGHER HYDE
SY 851902 DWT
54 hectare of heathland with areas of bog and wet woodland. Rich flora and insect fauna - outstanding site for dragonflies. Access from roadside on minor Wareham-Puddletown road near ARC buildings south-east of Gallows Hill.

HOD HILL
ST 857107 NT
32 hectare comprising large iron age hillfort renowned for downland flora and fauna, particularly butterflies. Access from lay-by on Child Okeford-Steepleton House road at ST 853113 or by footpath from Havelins, Stourpaine village where there is limited parking.

HOG CLIFF
SY 620976 EN
88 hectare National Nature Reserve of chalk grassland, scrub and coppice woodland in 3 separate blocks astride the A37 east of Maiden Newton. Access limited to public foot and bridle paths from Maiden Newton or from A37 at South Field Hill. (SY 620972)

HOLT HEATH
SU 060040 NT/EN
483 hectare National Nature Reserve. Third largest heath in Dorset, north west of Wimborne. Includes 72 hectare woodlands (Holt Wood and Holt Forest) separate from heath. Heathland restoration project at White Sheet Plantation. Limited parking on minor road from Holt to Three-Legged Cross and at White Sheet Forest car park off Broom Hill-Holt road at SZ 048038. Several tracks across heath for foot access.

HOLTON HEATH
SY 955910 EN
117 hectare National Nature Reserve of heathland with birch and Scots Pine wood. Extends to north shore of Poole Harbour. With reedbed and saltmarsh. Heathland restoration continues. Access restricted due to safety hazards on site of former explosives factory.

HOLWAY WOODS
ST 633200 DWT
16 hectare of mixed deciduous woodland and rough grassland. Access by permissive footpath. North of Sherborne. No easy parking nearby.

HURN FOREST RESERVES
SU 104015-SZ 135991 DWT
Seven distinct reserves totalling 87 hectare and covering a range of heathland habitats - mature dry heath, wet heath, bog, and willow carr, meadows and copses. Within Moors River flood plain and Hurn Forest (Forest Enterprise). Forest paths. Convenient access to Forest from Matchams Lane car park 1.5 miles north of Hurn village at SZ 128989.

KIMMERIDGE BAY
See Purbeck Marine Wildlife Reserve

KINGCOMBE MEADOWS
SY 545985 DWT
152 hectare farmland reserve untouched by modern agricultural practices. Superb unploughed and unsprayed grassland with ancient hedgerows, scrub and mature trees. Small woodlands with old coppice stools. Ancient green lanes. River Hooke and several streams and ponds. Exceptionally rich in grasses, herbs, lichens, butterflies and fungi. Visitor Centre at Pound Cottage in Lower Kingcombe hamlet. Small car park here (SY 554990). Also limited parking at Clift (SY 546984). Approach off A356 Maiden Newton-Crewkerne road through Toller Porcorum. Visitors welcome but access subject to farm management.

KINGSETTLE WOOD
ST 865255 WT
21 hectare wood on top of steep ridge north of Shaftesbury. Ancient woodland site previously replanted with conifers. Being returned to broadleaved wood. High beech forest, sycamore and ash. Plateau alder wood an unusual feature. Very limited parking off A350 (farm and lodge access must not be blocked). Paths from entrance in north-east corner of wood.

LODMOOR
SY 686810 RSPB
61 hectare wetland behind Weymouth seafront. Sea Life Centre, Butterfly Farm and Country Park adjoin. Low-lying grassland with shallow pools and fringed by reedbeds and scrub. Fine area for breeding, passage and wintering birds. 3 viewing hides on perimeter path. Access from large car park by Sea Life Centre off A353.

LOSCOMBE
SY 506982 DWT
10 hectare steeply sloping pasture, hedgerows, sunken lane, stream and small wetland rich in marsh orchids. Park in field opposite Rose cottage. Foot access by public footpath.

LULWORTH AND ARMY RANGES
Cove SY 827798 PRIVATE
Tyneham SY 882802 MOD
Lulworth Cove famous for geology and marine life. Also base for surrounding coastal downlands west towards White Nothe.

Warden and guided walks. Access by Coast Path from large car park at Cove. Visitor Centre.

Army Ranges cover over 2000 hectare from Lulworth east almost to Kimmeridge and include Tyneham, Flower's Barrow and Worbarrow Bay. Superb stretch of coastline and unimproved grassland rich in birds and butterflies including Lulworth skipper. Access from Kimmeridge,
Tyneham and Lulworth, all with car parks. Foot access restricted to waymarked paths for safety reasons. Visitor Centre at Tyneham. Viewpoint car park on Whiteway Hill. Open periods confined to most weekends and peak summer. Details of open/closed times publicised locally.

MAIDEN CASTLE
SY 668885 EH
Prominent hillfort south-west of Dorchester. Rich site for butterflies on banks and surrounds. Access from car park at SY 669889.

MELBURY DOWN
See Fontmell Down

MOORS VALLEY COUNTRY PARK AND FOREST
SU 106047 EDDC/FE
Over 500 hectare of coniferous woodland adjoining Country Park. Good facilities for wildlife viewing including tree top trail. Visitor Centre and large car park. Wardens, waymarked trails and events. Approach from Horton road 2 miles west of A31/A338 roundabout west of Ringwood.

MORDEN BOG
SY 915910 EN
149 hectare National Nature Reserve of botanically rich acid bog and surrounding heathland, one of the largest valley mires in England. Enclosed by Wareham Forest. Cattle grazed in joint project with Forest Enterprise. Foot access by forest paths. Main car park off Wareham-Bere Regis road. Alternative approach from Sherford Bridge on B3075 Morden road north of Sandford. See also Wareham Forest listing.

MUCKLEFORD
SY 642931 DWT
2.5 hectare disused chalk pit with rich grassland flora. Approach from A37 between Stratton and Grimstone. Parking alongside bridleway which gives foot access.

PIDDLES WOOD
See Girdlers Coppice & Piddles Wood

POOLE HARBOUR
VARIOUS
Magnificent estuary for wildlife. Accessible points for observing birdlife include path from Evening Hill, Lilliput to Sandbanks, Harbour entrance at Shell Bay, viewing hide on Studland Heath overlooking Brands Bay, Shipstal Point at Arne, Upton Country Park hides overlooking Holes Bay, Hamworthy Park, and Parkstone Bay local nature reserve (PBC) from Whitecliff recreation ground. Parking at or near these locations. Harbour cruises, including RSPB birdboats recommended. See also Brownsea Island.

PORTLAND
SY 690720 VARIOUS
Rich 'isle' for wildlife with cliffs and old quarries providing a variety of habitats. Bird observatory and ringing station at Portland Bill, landfall and departure of migrant birds. Cliff nesting sea birds. Butterfly reserve at Broadcroft Quarry. Guided walks. Large car park at Portland Bill SY676683.

POWERSTOCK COMMON
SY 540973 DWT
115 hectare ancient woodland site with coppice, heathy grassland, old hedgebanks and ponds. Exceptional site for butterflies. Wide range of flora and fauna. Old brick kiln and disused railway line add variety. Parking at SY 547973. Foot access on public footpaths and forest tracks.

PRESTON WILDLIFE GARDEN

SY 690830 DWT

Demonstration wildlife garden with both formal and natural areas. Access from entrance to Garden Centre on Littlemoor Road off A353 at Preston, Weymouth.

PUDDLETOWN FOREST

SY 740930 FE

Large coniferous forest to west of Puddletown. Car parks on Rhododendron Mile road south of A35 near Puddletown. Largest at Beacon Hill corner SY 746935. Forest walks. See also Thorncombe Wood and Blackheath listing.

PURBECK MARINE WILDLIFE RESERVE

SY 905792 DWT

Britain's first voluntary marine reserve. Extends from Clavell's Hard past Kimmeridge Bay towards Lulworth. Focal point is Kimmeridge Bay with underwater nature trail for divers and Visitor Centre with marine aquaria. Ideal at low tide for observing seashore life. Warden-led walks and seashore activities especially for children. Land privately owned. Approach via toll road to cliff-top car park.

RADIPOLE LAKE

SY 675798 RSPB/WPBC

78 hectare bird reserve in heart of Weymouth. Former estuary now a freshwater lake after dam built. Extensive reed beds and shallow pools. Much scrub along causeways and relict saltmarsh. Famous for breeding reed, sedge, and grasshopper warblers, with Cetti's warblers in scrub. Lake is important wintering area for wildfowl. Over 250 species of birds recorded, and 200 species of plants. Visitor Centre and nature trail. Bird hide. Approach from north end of public Swannery car park.

SOPLEY COMMON

SZ 132975 DWT

33 hectare dry and wet heathland with scrubby woodland and several ponds. Noted for reptiles and dragonflies. Parking in layby opposite garden nursery at SZ 129971 near Hurn village.

SOVELL DOWN

ST 992108 DWT

1.5 hectare remnant of chalk down with scrub on the Ackling Dyke with rich flora and butterflies. Limited parking on roadside at ST 994109. Access by bridleway.

SPYWAY FARM & SEACOMBE

SY 984770 - SY 999778 NT

Sea cliffs and coastal grassland on the southern Purbeck coast. Rich limestone flora including early spider orchid, and variety of butterflies. Grazing to restore turf continuing. Also seabird colonies. Includes Dancing Ledge, Blackers Hole and Seacombe. Car park and Visitor Centre at Spyway Barn, Langton Matravers SY 999778. Foot access also along Dorset coast path from Swanage and St Albhelm's Head.

STANPIT MARSH

SZ 170920 CBC

49 hectare estuary marshland reserve, important for wildfowl and waders. Approach from Stanpit Lane car park. Foot access on right of way only.

STOBOROUGH HEATH

See Hartland Moor

STUDLAND HEATH

SZ 030845 NT/EN

633 hectare National Nature Reserve extending from Shell Bay to Studland golf course and embracing Studland and Godlingston heaths, the Little Sea, Studland Bay and the southern shore of Brands Bay. Renowned for its sand dunes, dry and wet heathland, woodland and lakes. All British reptiles present. Rich

dragonfly location. Visitor Centre at Knoll Beach. Wildlife Information Centre off ferry road at SZ 027843. Bird hides around Little Sea and facing Brands Bay. Wardens, guided walks and nature trails. 3 NT car parks at Studland and one at Shell Bay.

TADNOLL

SY 792873 DWT

44 hectare reserve of varied heathland and wet meadows on western edge of Winfrith Heath. Park at reserve entrance SY 792873. Access by permissive path.

THORNCOMBE WOOD & BLACK HEATH

SY 726922 DCC

26 hectare mixed woodland and heath on west side of Puddletown Forest (see listing above). Waymarked trails. Access from car park south of A35 near Higher Bockhampton.

TOWNSEND

SZ 024782 DWT

16 hectare limestone grassland. Rich in calcareous flowers including early spider orchid. Scrub-filled hollows of disused quarries contrast with dry stony banks. Bats hibernate in underground quarries. Approach from residential district between Swanage and Herston. Roadside parking nearby.

TROUBLEFIELD

SZ 125978 DWT

6 hectare rich wet grassland by Moors River near Hurn Airport. Great variety of dragonflies. Damp deciduous woodland attractive for birds. Limited car parking.

TURNWORTH

ST 810085 NT

54 hectare of old deciduous woodland and unimproved downland. Access on foot along ridgeway from Okeford Hill picnic site car park ST 812093. Convenient

also for visiting Bonsley Common and Shillingstone Forest.

UPTON COUNTRY PARK
SY 995930 PBC
22.3 hectare country park on western side of Poole. Farmland, woodland, lakes and saltmarsh/mudflats fringing Holes Bay as well as formal gardens. Park managed for conservation. Good opportunities for wildlife viewing including bird hides. Visitor Centre, waymarked trails, wardens, events. Ample car parking near entrance off A35.

WAREHAM FOREST
SY 905895 FE
Major coniferous forest north of Wareham, noted for sika deer and birds of prey. Some old plantations being felled to restore heathland. Part of long-term project to increase wildlife value of the forest and Morden Bog (see listing above) which forest encloses. Sika Trail and other waymarked routes. Education Centre, rangers and events. Main car park on Wareham - Bere Regis road at map ref. above. Smaller walkers' car parks on this road and on B3075 Sandford - Morden road. Foot access on forest tracks.

WEST BEXINGTON
SY 527866 DWT
20 hectare shingle beach, reed bed, wet meadow and scrub area toward western end of Chesil Beach. Beach car park at West Bexington from B3157 at Swyre.

WHITE NOTHE & RINGSTEAD BAY
SY 765810 NT
182 hectare including White Nothe Cliff and Burning Cliff. Fine chalk grassland around White Nothe. Access from South Down car park above Ringstead at SY 760824.

RECORDING DORSET'S WILDLIFE
In 1975 a biological recording centre was set up in Dorchester known as the Dorset Environment Records Centre (DERC). This was a joint project between the County Council, the Dorset Naturalists' Trust and Dorset County Museum and its aim was to gather as much data as possible about the flora and fauna of the county, initially on record cards. It is now a limited company with a staff of three and is supported by the County and District Councils, the Dorset Wildlife Trust, the Dorset Natural History and Archaeological Society and English Nature and partly funded by its own contract work.

DERC has now computerised 225,000 species records and publishes a newsletter, annual report, and many useful publications, such as *Endangered Wildlife in Dorset*. Its records are used by many organisations and its presence is essential for the scientific basis of nature conservation in the county. The Records Centre is now based at County Hall and welcomes accurate wildlife records for its database.

FINALLY AN INVITATION

If you have learned from this book more about Dorset's rich wildlife treasures and been inspired by the beauty and variety of the natural world on our doorstep please lend your support by joining the Dorset Wildlife Trust. Full details and a membership form can be obtained from:

Dorset Wildlife Trust
Brooklands Farm, Forston
Dorchester, Dorset DT2 7AA

Telephone: 01305 264620